URSULA FRANKLIN is a member of the Department of Foreign Languages at Grand Valley State Colleges, Allendale, Michigan, and author of *An Anatomy of Poesis: The Prose Poems of Stéphane Mallarmé*.

While Paul Valéry's lyric poetry, as well as his dialogues, dramatic work, and critical prose, have preoccupied his critics, his prose poems have been virtually ignored and his position in the tradition of the genre has remained unacknowledged. This study demonstrates the significance of Valéry as a prose poet and of the form and its evolution in the poet's *oeuvre*. The close textual reading and analysis concentrate on Valéry's prose *aubades* – the prose poems, poetic prose fragments, and sequences celebrating the emergence of the self and its world at dawn.

The theme of dawn pervades Valéry's poetry from the opening chord of *Charmes* to those Notebooks which he kept for almost half a century and which are the source of so much of his poetry. This book shows how the moment and theme of dawn have also inspired the greater part of Valéry's prose poems and poetic prose fragments.

Critics have begun to show interest in the break-up of traditional genres and in the emergence of the fragment as a new literary form. But Valéry's position in this development has so far escaped critical inquiry, as have his prose poems in general. Professor Franklin redresses the balance with rigor, poise, and elegance. She shows how Valéry's artistic progression from the traditional prose poem to the fragment, the evolution of the *recueil* to the sequence, represents a development very similar to that manifest in another new prose form, the new *nouveau roman*. It is a brilliant analysis of a neglected aspect of Valéry's work and a thoughtful interpretation of Valéry's thought and poetics as a whole.

URSULA FRANKLIN

The Rhetoric
of Valéry's
Prose *Aubades*

UNIVERSITY OF TORONTO PRESS

Toronto Buffalo London

Library of Congress Cataloging in Publication Data

Franklin, Ursula.
 The rhetoric of Valéry's prose aubades.

 Bibliography: p.
 Includes index.
 1. Valéry, Paul, 1871-1945 – Style.   2. Prose Poems,
French – History and criticism.   3. Dawn in literature.
I. Title.
 PQ2643.A26Z613   841'.9'12   78-13044
 ISBN 0-8020-5427-7

For J.A.Y.

Contents

PREFACE   ix

1   Introduction   3
2   'Purs Drames'   10
3   Fragments   20
4   The Trilogy 'A B C'   32
5   'Trois Réveils'   43
6   Three 'Matins'   52
7   'Reprise'   62
8   'Notes d'Aurore'   72
9   'Moments'   78
10   Petits Poèmes abstraits   87
11   'Méditation avant pensée'   107
12   'La Considération matinale'   112
13   'A Grasse'   114
14   Conclusion   122

NOTES   133

BIBLIOGRAPHY   148

INDEX   152

Preface

This study, which deals with a long-neglected area of the poetic universe of Paul Valéry, is a detailed analysis of a group of prose poems, undertaken with the intent of showing the significance of the genre to the poet, as well as his leading role in its evolution.

In my exploration of Valéry's poetry, I have been greatly indebted to the work of James R. Lawler. And I owe much to the poet's other commentators, to Ned Bastet, Nicole Celeyrette-Pietri, Christine Crow, Jean Levaillant, Huguette Laurenti, Octave Nadal, Judith Robinson, and many who must remain unnamed. Robert Greer Cohn has my special gratitude for reading the manuscript, for his invaluable suggestions and encouragement.

I thank the editors of *The Centennial Review*, the *Kentucky Romance Quarterly*, and *The Michigan Academician* for their kind permission to use material which first appeared in their journals.

This book has been published with the help of grants from the Canadian Federation for the Humanities, using funds provided by the Social Sciences and Humanities Research Council of Canada, and from the Andrew W. Mellon Foundation to the University of Toronto Press. My thanks go to Dr R.M. Schoeffel of University of Toronto Press for all his help. I have quoted extensively from the poetry and prose of Valéry by kind permission of the copyright holders, Editions Gallimard, Paris.

Finally, this study could not have been completed without the untiring advice of my friend and teacher, John A. Yunck, to whom it is appropriately dedicated.

UF

THE RHETORIC OF VALÉRY'S PROSE AUBADES

'J'étais fait pour chanter Matines'
Paul Valéry, *Lettres à quelques-uns*

1   Introduction

While Paul Valéry's lyric poetry, as well as his dialogues, dramatic work, and critical prose, have continuously preoccupied his critics, the poet's prose poems have received little attention.[1] Valéry's major position in the tradition of the genre has so far been overlooked; Suzanne Bernard in her monumental *Le Poème en prose de Baudelaire jusqu'à nos jours*, for example, mentions the poet merely in passing.[2] In this study I propose to demonstrate the significance of Valéry the prose poet, as well as that of the prose poem and its evolution in his poetic universe. My reading will concentrate on Valéry's aubades; the prose poems, poetic fragments, and sequences celebrating the emergence of the self and its world at dawn.

Dawn is Valéry's privileged moment, a moment between night and day when the self and the world are pure imminence, pure essence, pure virtuality:

> Au réveil, si douce la lumière ... le mot "Pur" ouvre mes lèvres. Le
> jour qui jamais encore ne fut, les pensées, le *tout en germe*
> considéré sans obstacle – le Tout qui s'ébauche dans l'or et que
> nulle chose particulière ne corrompt encore. Le Tout est commence-
> ment. En germe le plus haut degré universel.[3]

'L'Aurore' becomes the golden and mythic Eden 'au commencement,' at the beginning of a world whose words and figures, whose reality, is but a falling off from that former state. The theme of dawn, therefore, pervades Valéry's poetry from the opening chord of the *Charmes* to some of the great dialogues. Daybreak, moreover, is the moment of Valéry's *Cahiers*, those notebooks which were Narcissus' constant mirror for half a century, and which are the spring and inexhaustible source of so much of his poetry. Both the moment and the theme of dawn have also inspired the greater part of Valéry's prose poems, for it is this *Ursprache* of poetry, this 'poésie brute,' antecedent to formulation and regulation in traditional rhyme and meter, which is suited to sing most ardently the beginning – 'Au commencement.'

The prose poem as a literary genre was firmly established by Valéry's nineteenth-century predecessors, and the autonomy of both the *poème en prose* and its frame, the *recueil*, was consecrated with the posthumous publication in 1869 of Baudelaire's *Spleen de Paris*. From this point on, many poets venture into the new genre which, according to Baudelaire, introduces a modern accent into lyricism:

> Quel est celui de nous qui n'a pas, dans ses jours d'ambition, rêvé le miracle d'une prose poétique, musicale sans rythme et sans rime, assez souple et assez heurtée pour s'adapter aux mouvements lyriques de l'âme, aux ondulations de la rêverie, aux soubresauts de la conscience?[4]

My reading of Valéry's morning prose poems reveals a poetic prose language of the greatest musicality and suppleness, an instrument rendering harmoniously both the 'mouvements lyriques de l'âme' and the 'soubresauts de la conscience.' The lyric movements of the matutinal *moi*'s soul and consciousness in fact constitute these poems' major theme and melody.

The young Valéry's *maître*, Mallarmé, inherited and expanded the 'poème en prose' to include the 'poème critique,' manifest, for example, in the early 'Symphonie Littéraire,' one of whose pieces is a tribute to Baudelaire. The prose poem preoccupied Mallarmé throughout his creative life, from the early pieces of 1864 to 1893. He published his prose poems first separately in various reviews from 1864 to 1887, then together in *Pages* of 1891, and finally incorporated them into a cycle of thirteen prose poems under the title 'Anecdotes ou poëmes' in *Divagations* (1897).[5] Between April and June 1880 Rimbaud's 'Illuminations' appeared, first in five issues of *La Vogue*, then in book form, presented by Verlaine, in 1886. And these dizzying 'coloured plates,' defying both traditional vision and form, created a new kind of pure poetry that impetuously revolutionized the still young prose poem.[6]

It was the almost simultaneous encounter with Mallarmé's and Rimbaud's prose poems that decisively influenced Valéry's first attempts in the genre. In 1889 Valéry had read Huysmans' *A Rebours*, which immediately became his 'livre de chevet.' Not merely did *A Rebours* sing the praises of the prose poem – 'de toutes les formes de la littérature, celle du poème en prose était la forme préférée de des Esseintes' – but it drew attention to Mallarmé's poetry, and especially his early prose poems.[7] The youthful Valéry sums up his impression of *A Rebours*: 'En somme c'est pour moi, et je me *sers* souvent de ce livre, une suite de très beaux poèmes en prose très nerveux.'[8] He paid a fitting tribute to Huysmans by means of one of his own earliest prose poems, the posthumously published 'Les Vieilles Ruelles,' which he wrote in 1889, when he was eighteen years old. Shortly thereafter, he published 'Purs Drames,' a prose poem which he republished in 1931, and which he retrospectively considered an important event of 1892. With 'Purs Drames' the Valéryan prose poem comes into its own; the piece already foreshadows, moreover, the aubades which will make up the largest group of these poems.

From 1898 on, Valéry mentions in his letters to Gide a 'conte' he was planning to write about the gradual alterations of the mind as it falls into sleep and dream. But he predicts even then that this tale, which he entitled 'Agathe,' would never be finished. The piece is soon afterwards envisaged as a fragment, which Valéry thinks of incorporating in the Teste cycle as 'l'intérieur de la nuit de M. Teste.' The text, published posthumously in 1956, longer than any other Valéryan prose poem, is neither a *conte*, nor an 'histoire brisée,' as it lacks both fiction and characters in the traditional sense; 'Agathe' is a poetic text, a prose poem which already points to the further evolution of that genre and its breaking up into the poetic prose fragment.[9]

Critics have begun to show interest in the emergence of the 'fragment,' but Valéry's position in this development – an evolution which paradoxically appears to be a dissolution of form, from poem or *conte* to an almost archaeologically obscure literary shard – has so far escaped critical inquiry, as have his prose poems in general.[10] There is a marked morphological change from the anecdotal or narrative form of prose poem, situated in a structured, or at least unified, *recueil* or cycle, to the shard-like, fragmented quality of the Valéryan prose poems, some of them centred on a mere moment in time, which are dispersed throughout his work. The break-up of the genre, moreover, from a diachronic point of view is reflected not merely in the prose poem itself, but also in the disappearance of its frame, the 'recueil.'

Valéry never grouped his prose poems together into a *recueil*; he frequently placed them into sequences or series, and individual pieces as well as some of the sequences appear under such headings as 'Mélange,' 'Poésie brute,' 'Tel Quel,' and 'Morceaux choisis,' along with free verse, sketches, observations and epigrams, or dreams. The form of the Valéryan prose poem is, besides, much more varied than that of any of his predecessors.

In almost every one of Mallarmé's 'Anecdotes ou poëmes' a short narrative or 'récit' constitutes the vehicle for the poem's symbolic meaning. On the contrary, though some of Valéry's prose poems are narrative in this sense (as for example the well-known 'Enfance aux cygnes'), most of them have a momentary, 'broken' quality about them, indicated by such titles as 'Instants' and 'Histoires brisées.' I shall be using the terms 'broken,' 'momentary,' or 'instantaneous' frequently to denote this characteristic of Valéry's prose poems: the quality which isolates and freezes into poetry the single, detached moment, somewhat in the manner that a still camera, its shutter open only for a fragment of a second, isolates the vision of that instant and records it on film. Most of Valéry's prose poems are sparkling fragments of an interior mono-dialogue, brilliant verbal reflections of the poet's momentary states of mind, or of his vision of the phenomena surrounding him.

If we should very roughly group Valéry's prose poems into narrative pieces, descriptive poems, and those celebrating a state of mind – before considering a thematic grouping such as 'water prose poems,' 'poems of the city,' and 'morning pieces' – we would find the majority of the poems falling under the last group, that is the prose poems objectifying an 'état d'esprit.'

Most of the prose poems celebrating the awakening of the self and of the world at dawn – the largest thematic group – combine the 'descriptive,' the painting of dawn, with the objectification of the persona's 'état d'esprit,' Baudelaire's 'soubresauts de la conscience.' These poems are a dialectic of the self with the self, *je* to *moi*, as it rediscovers its body and the world, and they capture the moment when 'mon corps, mon esprit' and 'mon monde' – Valéry's 'trois points cardinaux de connaissance' (c I, p 1142) – come together to form the beginning of a new day. The fact that the early morning hours, devoted to the *Cahiers*, were Valéry's privileged time of day accounts not merely for the surprising volume of the aubades, but also for their persistence in the *oeuvre* throughout the poet's life, from 'Purs Drames' (1892) to the year of his death. Many of these morning prose poems were published posthumously, and a large number of them were found in the *Cahiers*; Valéry himself published many of his prose aubades in the twenties, at the time when the theme of 'aurore' is also prominent in *Charmes* and in some of the dialogues.

While 'Purs Drames,' all its uniqueness and originality of vision notwithstanding, still represents structurally the traditional prose poem, some of the later aubades reveal a new form. The prose poem 'Matin' which Valéry published in 1927 in *Autres Rhumbs* (o II, pp 658-9), for example, consists of three parts and opens with three lines of free verse. The first section renders the self's awakening to the privileged moment of 'Purs Drames':

> Au réveil, si douce la lumière et beau ce bleu vivant!
> Le mot "Pur" ouvre mes lèvres.

The second part presents the persona's reflections at this moment:

> Que ne puis-je retarder d'être moi...
> Pourquoi, ce matin, me choisirais-je?

And the third section celebrates the state of imminence of the self and of the world with its rising sun:

> L'âme boit aux sources une gorgée de liberté et de *commencement sans conditions.*
> Cet azur est une Certitude. Ce Soleil qui paraît ... s'annonce et monte comme un juge...

The poem's three fragments make up the whole. But a slightly different version of the poem's first part, combined with a fragment of its second part, had already appeared in one of the 1913 *Cahiers* (c II, pp 1261-2). This recombining of various fragments of a given prose poem to form another is frequent in Valéry and characteristic of his creative technique. It is the phenomenon to which I will frequently refer by the term 'mobile fragment.' One is reminded that the opening and closing poems of *Charmes*, 'Aurore' and 'Palme,' were one at one stage of their growth, and that 'La Jeune Parque' gradually grew out of its constituent fragments, not unlike the 'Fragments du Narcisse.'[11]

In 1925, Valéry published in *Commerce* the prose poems 'A B C,' indicating on the title-page: 'trois lettres extraites d'un alphabet à paraître.' This 'alphabet' was never completed, and the three prose poems, 'extracted' from a projected larger whole, constitute a trilogy, a series of three pieces, each one complete, but all sequentially related in developing a single theme: in 'A' the mind finds its body upon awakening at dawn; in 'B' mind and body unite as the self arises to a new day; and in 'C' the united self takes possession of the world unfolding before it. But subsequent to their publication in *Commerce*, Valéry separated the poem's 'fragments.' A modified version of 'A' appears in a free-verse rendition in the 'Poèmes' section of *Histoires brisées*, and he republished 'C' under the title 'Comme le Temps est calme' separately in 1930 in *Morceaux choisis*. The fragments, 'A, B,' and 'C,' then, form one prose poem of three parts, but the parts also exist as mobile fragments, each a separate prose poem, but each potentially a part of a new pattern, like glittering stones which can be used repeatedly in various mosaics.[12]

In 1932, Valéry published in *La Revue de France* a series of four prose poems: 'I. Avant toute Chose,' 'II. L'Unique,' 'III. Accueil du jour,' 'IV. La Rentrée'; and in 1939 the three-part prose poem 'Méditation avant pensée' (o I, pp 351-2) appeared in *Mélange*. 'I. Avant toute Chose' and 'Méditation I' are the same piece, the fragment serving in both sequences as the opening. From the same period dates a six-part prose poem sequence entitled 'Moments' (o I, pp 311-13), whose first fragment comprises a six-line free-verse section. This poem's second fragment, already composed in its final form in a 1920-1 *Cahier* (c II, p 1272), is a characteristic example of the Valéryan prose poem, the poetic prose fragment which captures the fleeting moment – the title of the sequence is 'Moments' – between night and dawn when the *moi* meets its world:

> Aube – Ce n'est pas l'aube. Mais le déclin de la lune, perle rongée, glace fondante, et une lueur mourante à qui le jour naissant se substitue peu à peu – J'aime ce moment si pur, final, initial. Mélange de calme, de renoncement, de négation...

The same moment, painted with the same images, is objictified in the third part of the 'A B C' poem(s):

> Quelque oranger respire là dans l'ombre. Il subsiste très haut peu de fines étoiles à l'extrême de l'aigu. La lune est ce fragment de glace fondante...

These fragments then, and even parts of them – phrases and images – are mobile within the *œuvre* which contains them. The 'fragment' by definition affirms the principle of unity on which it depends; and this unity is Valéry's total poetic universe. In the *Ego Scriptor*, he says, 'or cette oeuvre toute mienne se réduit à des poèmes, à des fragments...' (c I, p 306), and about the *Cahiers*, 'si je prends des fragments dans ces cahiers ... l'ensemble fera quelque chose. Le lecteur – et même moi-même – en formera une *unité*' (c I, p 10). Valéry's poetic prose fragments, like the 'Fragments du Narcisse,' the *recitativos* of 'La Jeune Parque,' or the stanzas of 'Le Cimetière marin' are internal mono-dialogues – 'à la base, le dialogue intérieur,' says the *ego scrip-*

tor (c I, p 300) – poetic explorations of a *moi* both subjective and universal. And the prose poems, poetic fragments, and sequences of dawn – the aubades – celebrate the genesis of both the subject and the universe.

The study which follows is essentially a close reading of Valéry's major morning prose fragments and sequences, in the context of his *œuvre*. I have not attempted to be exhaustive, but have analyzed in detail those aubades which best reflect the essential aspects of the poet's vision of dawn, and which are most characteristic of the poet in their architectonics. In regard to their context, I have demonstrated at some length how these representative fragments are related to the major themes and motifs of Valéry's other prose and verse.

2 'Purs Drames'

Valéry published his first prose aubade, 'Purs Drames' (o i, pp 1597-9), in 1892, and in a letter of the same year he thanks Gide for 'des mots délicieux sur mes Drames.'[1] This prose poem remained important to the poet, for he republished it in 1931, when he was at the height of his fame. 'Purs Drames' was republished in 1957 by Octave Nadal, who views it as Valéry's first characteristic expression in the genre:

> Purs drames annonce, en effet, dès 1892, l'écriture proprement valéryenne du poème en prose, reconnaissable, en dehors de ses caractères intrinsèques, à l'accord du nouveau motif d'ordre universel (celui d'une pensée remontée à ses indices) avec la plénitude d'une forme rythmique épurée jusqu'à la transparence. Il est le premier d'un ensemble de poèmes plus achevés sans doute, mais apparentés entre eux par l'invention structurale – symétrie des figures du rythme et de la syntaxe, continuité musicale, couleur particulière des timbres.[2]

During the previous year Valéry had met Mallarmé, and that poet's verse is repeatedly the subject of his correspondence, which also mentions Rimbaud – who had died in November 1891 – and Poe. But it is especially the prose poems of the two latter writers that fascinated Valéry. In a letter to Gide of March 1892, the same month in which 'Purs Drames' appeared, Valéry writes: 'Je suis au fond d'*Eureka* et des Illuminations.'[3] And it is this background of Mallarméan verse and Rimbaud's *Illuminations* which provides the poetic setting of 'Purs Drames.'

'Pur' is a key term of Valéry's poetic and metapoetic, as well as his discursive language. From 1892 on he uses the word so frequently to designate his aspirations – 'le moi pur,' 'la poésie pure' – that it has come to denote his distinctive characteristic. Books have been written about 'la pureté de Valéry,' a notion as obvious as 'the idealism of Plato' or 'the hermeticism of Mallarmé.'[4] Because the word is so multivalent in Valéry, it behooves us to examine its specific intent in the title of our poem, where 'pur' has again several meanings, designating a pure vision of an innocent, pure world, objectified in pure poetry. But then the notion of poetic vision objectified – implying stasis – is followed by the kinetic term 'drame,' emphasizing movement and change, rather than immutability. 'Purs Drames' celebrates becoming, the *de-venir* of a world – be it of the imagination, of reality, or of surreality – set forth in the imagery of sight. 'Un œil pur' is the protagonist of the 'drame' about to unfold. And the eye is the poem's hero in a twofold sense since the piece both is, and is about, a vision; a vision which we recreate, moreover, by our eye, as we behold its *écriture*.

The opening phrase 'les sites sont ornés de pudiques bijoux, qui scintillent' in using the term 'site' – a Renaissance painting term designating 'un paysage considéré du point de vue de l'esthétique, du pittoresque' (Robert) – places the emphasis on the eye by alluding to the visual art. And like the painter, the poet will compose, rather than describe, his tableau. In a much later prose poem, 'Composition d'un port,' Valéry says: 'un langage ... conviendra pour célébrer (non décrire, qui est une triste besogne) tout ce qui encombre la vue...' (o II, p 860).

Our 'sites adorned with chaste gems gleaming' evoke the symbolist garden, the 'paysage d'âme,' and favourite setting of symbolist poetry. We encounter it in some of Valéry's verse poems of that time: in the 'jardin mélodieux' of 'La Fileuse' (1891); in 'Féerie' (1890) with its 'lys et des roses neigeuses' among the marble of lunar fountains; in 'Les Vaines Danseuses' (1891) with 'de mauves et d'iris et de mourantes roses.' In a letter to Gide of March 1891, Valéry writes: 'Le jardin symbolique s'ouvre à nos pas, fleuri, parfumé. On n'en sort plus.'[5] But in our poem's garden, the flowers have become chaste gems, and their transformation into mineral purity brings to mind Rimbaud's 'herbages d'acier et d'émeraude' of 'Mystique' or the 'pièces d'or jaune semées sur l'agate, des piliers d'acajou supportant un dome d'émeraudes' of 'Fleurs' in the *Illuminations*.[6]

But then, in the following sentence-paragraph, the garden is transcended, as the eye moves to a cosmic vision of the world turning in its vast sleep. And the earth's rhythmic rotation is stylistically suggested by the regularity of the iambic and anapestic rhythms in the inverted sentence: 'au silence, au soleil, à l'ombre, si le Monde se retourne dans son vaste sommeil...' The strong rhythm emphasizes the repetition of the three parallel prepositional phrases preceding the subject, the world, which we are thus beholding as from a distance. Then, immediately afterward, the dark vowels of the phrase, evocative of cosmic night, are 'illuminated' by flashes of light vowels, still phrased in that free and fluent combination of anapests and iambs: 'l'éclair d'une parure illumine ce geste obscur.' 'L'éclair d'une parure' echoes the 'bijoux qui scintillent,' and this vision of the earth throwing off a mysterious gleam as it revolves in the dark immensity of the universe is reminiscent of Mallarmé's '...au lointain de cette nuit, la Terre/Jette d'un grand éclat l'insolite mystère.'[7]

Then the vision contracts from the cosmic to the terrestrial, to focus on the phenomena gradually revealed by the break of dawn. Clouds, dew-drops, the rush, calixes of flowers – 'et pierreries' – weeds' tall stems, and 'la douce figure humaine' are caught in the movement of awakening to the first day of the world. For everything in this garden, which is Eden, stirs with life and desire: ' – Ecumes, – aventureuses nues qu'effleure une plume, avec des gouttes ... – mains ailées ... dont le désir d'abeilles ou d'astres á chiper, entreouvre et referme les calices ... la douce figure humaine, errante ... ' The young world is emerging like Venus from the sea foam; it is the beginning of all things, the birth of love and life, of *physis*, out of the *Urelement*, 'l'eau qui les mire.'

This Edenic vision recalls Rimbaud's 'Après le Déluge,' a world purified and renewed by and out of water: '...un lièvre s'arrête dans les sainfoins et les clochettes mouvantes, et dit sa prière à travers la toile d'araignée.[8] And our dawn's 'pierreries' echo the *Illumination*'s 'Aube,' where 'les pierreries regardèrent, et les ailes se levèrent sans bruit.'[9] In 'Purs Drames,' the symbolist garden, the theme of dawn – heralding Valéry's aubades – and the vision of Paradise are superimposed, to elaborate the myth of the return to the source.[10]

Finally the poet-persona introduces himself as 'un œil pur' and evokes and foresees the Fall – 'tous ces beaux débris d'une vérité tôt disparue par la foudre' – which is, at the same time, the death sentence of this dawn. Paradise will be lost, paradise is lost; and the persona points to the resurrective function of 'le Poète,' evoker of vision and creator of Fable, of the sublime lie which Mallarmé called 'l'explication Orphique de la terre.'[11] More than once Valéry insists

AU COMMENCEMENT ETAIT LA FABLE

Nécessairement...

Donc, si tu imagines remonter vers le "commencement," tu ne peux
l'imaginer qu'en te dépouillant, à chaque recul un peu plus, de ce
que tu sais par expérience, ou du moins par des témoignages qui se
font de plus en plus rares. Et tu es obligé pour concevoir ces tableaux
de plus en plus éloignés, de les compléter de plus en plus par ta
production propre de personnages, d'événements et de théâtres.

A la limite, il n'y a plus que du *toi*. C'est tout *du toi*: fable pure (o i,
p 394).[12]

The poet's matutinal eye, projecting its 'lueur lustrale' upon the
world's debris, sees in these fragments reminiscences of the original
unity of the universe. The underlying cosmogony here is a combination of Platonism – to which the poem will allude later on – of Poe's
Eureka, and that transformation of both which Baudelaire effected in
his 'Correspondances'-complex. The Poet's 'lustral eye' is one purified
as by baptismal water, that is an eye spiritually reborn; and in the
following sentence-paragraph, entirely devoted to the eye, the persona explains its sacramental ritual. The eye's 'vertu d'enfance [the
innocent vision] serait éphémère, s'il ne ruisselait chaque aurore
sur son miroir, à cause de quelque souriant mensonge, une eau
discrète de Larme.' This baptism by lacrimal water introduces the
Valéryan theme of 'la larme,' taken up repeatedly in both his prose
and verse. The poet devoted a whole lyric paragraph of 'La Jeune
Parque' to its exploration:

Larme qui fais trembler à mes regards humains
Une variété de funèbres chemins;
Tu procèdes de l'âme, orgueil du labyrinthe.
...
D'où nais-tu? Quel travail toujours triste et nouveau
Te tire avec retard, Larme, de l'ombre amère? (o i, p 104)

What is the tear? All tears, says Valéry, 'montent toujours d'un
manque. Mais il en est d'une espèce divine, qui naissent du manque
de la force de soutenir un objet divin de l'âme, d'en égaler et
épuiser l'essence' (o i, p 339).[13] In the *Cahiers* Valéry says about the
tears that come at dawn:

Le matin est mon séjour.
Il s'y trouve pour moi une tristesse sobre et transparente. ... Je suis

toujours à ce point de la journée, à demi percé quant au cœur de
je ne sais quel trait qui me ferait venir les Larmes sans cause – à demi
fou de lucidité sans objet – et d'une froide et implacable "tension de
compréhension" (c i, p 110).

In 'Purs Drames' the tears come 'à cause de quelque souriant mensonge,' which must be Mallarmé's sublime lie, the poetic fiction of an
intelligible universe. The eye is then represented as a mirror, a motif
taken up in the following section, in which the poet-persona almost
despairs of reviving the paradisiac vision: 'Ancienne vanité!' But one
must capture it surprised 'dans une flaque céleste, dont la glace
mince imite l'éther absolu, ou lucidement le pense.' This celestial
pool whose fine mirror imitates, that is reflects, the absolute ether –
the sky in its physical as well as metaphysical and metaphorical
sense – this celestial pool which *thinks* its images lucidly, is the Poet's
eye as mirror, reflecting both an outer and an inner world. 'Un œil
pur,' we have said, is the hero of 'Purs Drames.'[14]
    In the final section of the poem's italicized prelude, the poet-
persona invites us to 'indulge' in the vision – the poem – 'puisqu'il n'y
a plus, pour amuser les ombres, de Théâtre, – et, pour paraître au
seuil de cette platonicienne caverne, *personne*, sous le luminaire déjà
presque idéal.' Our fallen world, represented by the conventional
image of the Cave of Plato's simile, is contrasted with the one created
by the poem. In a world where myth and religion have died, 'il n'y a
plus de Théâtre,' except for 'le spectacle angélique' of 'Purs
Drames.' No one but the Poet appears on the threshold of the Cave to
tell of the sun, which is rising.
    And then the poem's scene unfolds as 'sous le luminaire déjà
presque idéal':

> d'une touffe de joncs sensibles, chevelure végétale où vibrent des
> insectes, jaillit dans les atomes d'or, joyau anonyme, énigmatique et
> seul, un bras de rose, fleuri d'une rêveuse main, dont à peine les
> doigts blancs s'agitent, d'un plaisir sous les verdures, ou d'un vœu,
> ou par la brise.

The 'luminaire déjà presque idéal' is both the morning sun and the
poet's visionary eye, illuminating and animating the world from on
high (the persona is looking down at his garden from a window),
giving life and movement – 'vibrer,' 'jaillir,' 's'agiter' – to its forms.
And these forms are seen as for the first time by an eye that is at once

passive and active, that both receives and creates them. Valéry frequently describes this process in the *Cahiers*:

> Il est de ma nature mentale de me trouver tout à coup *devant* les
> choses comme tout inconnues – et comme de mesurer du regard *toute*
> la distance entre elles et ce moi qui doit les subir ou accomplir, *sans le*
> *secours* de *l'habitude*, des *conventions*, des *moyens déjà connus* (c I, p
> 135).

The artist must 'wash' his eye, 'il doit ... faire effort pour nettoyer son
œil, et *voir* au lieu de lire' (c I, p 447). A tuft of rushes becomes a
'chevelure végétale,' and the flower is a nameless jewel. Its stem is a
'bras de rose,' its blossom 'une rêveuse main,' its petals are white
fingers stirring in the breeze, or from a secret desire. Thus mineral,
floral, and human shapes blend freely in the original garden, where
the world was one.

The first couple's 'pure Feet' graze the lips of 'speechless' flowers in
this impressionistic tableau, whose elements appear in the order of
their perception:

> Sur les bouches sans parole d'une foule rose de corolles, pas émue de
> cette indifférente course, des Pieds purs, ornements inférieurs d'un
> simple couple inaperçu, dont l'un fuit l'autre, féminin.

The poet-persona loves the grace of the moving line, 'je désire le
profil des fleurs et des membres très rapide,' the natural line subli-
mated to the ornamental: 'l'orteil figuré vaguement en volute.' And
in his temporal medium of language he captures the movement of
forms more readily than the painter, for not only does each sentence
– each brushstroke, or stroke of the pen – reproduce it, but the whole
poem *gradually* unfolds the garden as it comes into being at dawn:
'Une main d'eau ... s'allonge,' ... 'l'extrême papillon bat des ailes,' ...
's'évapore au calice du ciel, une nue,' ... 'Et voici! L'aube des
formes.'[15]

The transitional moment in its evanescence is imaged and symbolized by the divine glow-worms, 'ces phalènes divines, indifférentes
bientôt à chacune des joyeuses touffes.' These little stars which
bring back reminiscences of childhood – 'la saisir, la couver dans le
creux de mains puériles, courir, et rire de la tenir captive – une
Etoile!' – are the ideal and real *pierreries* of the young garden.

Only now does the persona reveal his 'point of view,' looking down
from his window obliquely upon a world 'sous la figure de la

croisée,' a world stirring to life and already threatened by death: 'on dirait que le jardin tremblant s'envole.' For its forms are not immutable, but in perpetual becoming: 'si les fleurs d'une minute jouent des ailes pour fuir, où irons-nous Idées? ... '

Finally the persona abandons the vision, as he turns his glance away from the garden outside the window to reflect on it. And here the poem becomes self-conscious and self-reflective, poetry about poetry, as its persona becomes its critic inside the poem itself. The images of 'Purs Drames' are not yet pure enough, for they are 'corrompues encore par la certitude de leurs éléments.' In a kind of ecstasy and *ivresse* – 'l'âme ivre d'elle-même' – the poet wants to reduce them, lead them back, restore them to simpler, that is purer, origins. 'Impur! qui désire une grimace ou la brutalité de cris; il n'importe que de deviner, et de mourir.' And Mallarmé's young disciple flirts dangerously here with the temptation of 'la pureté du Non-être' which haunted his master all his life.

Image is reduced to line, for 'il n'y a que les lignes simples pour faire pleurer le dur artiste, sans remords.' But at the same time, this ideal reduction alludes to the poem itself, 'les lignes simples' to its lines upon the white page. The twenty-two-year-old Mallarmé had similarly objectified that drama in creating 'un jeune paysage,' which a mere 'ligne d'azur mince et pâle' saves from nothingness:

> Imiter le Chinois au cœur limpide et fin
> De qui l'extase pure est de peindre la fin
> Sur ses tasses de neige à la lune ravie
> D'une bizarre fleur qui parfume sa vie
> Transparente, la fleur qu'il a sentie, enfant,
> Au filigrane bleu de l'âme se greffant.
> Et, la mort telle avec le seul rêve du sage,
> Serein, je vais choisir un jeune paysage
> Que je peindrais encor sur les tasses, distrait.
> Une ligne d'azur mince et pâle serait
> Un lac, parmi le ciel de porcelaine nue,
> Un clair croissant perdu par une blanche nue
> Trempe sa corne calme en la glace des eaux,
> Non loin de trois grands cils d'émeraude, roseaux.[16]

The prose poem's concluding paragraph begins with a short apostrophe reducing the entire poem – the reminiscence of Eden and the symbolic morning garden – to the line of dawn rising on the night sky: 'Aime donc le Drame pur d'une ligne sur l'espace de couleur céleste ou vitale.'[17] And this line is pure movement – 'elle n'existe qu'en mouvement beau' – and the ornament of life itself, 'l'ornement de toutes les vies.'

The poet no longer paints the attributes, or images, of dawn, but 'divines,' predicts and retraces, its essence ('il n'importe que de deviner ... Devine!'). For the ending – both the end and the telos – of the poem *is* that *esse*ntial pure line itself, traced out in the space of the page and the time of the period:

> elle se penche ensuite avec mélancolie, se noue, se concentre en spire – ou songe; file, et se laisse enfuir dans la joie d'une direction supérieure, se recourbe, habitude ou souvenir, puis rencontre au-delà de tous les astres, une Autre que d'inconnus destins distraient vers le même Occident, et ne terminera plus de fleurir, de disparaître dans la merveille du jeu, – éprise, diverse, monotone, – mince et noire.

'Slim and black' the *écriture* of this sentence flows and rhythmically (re)traces the movement which it signifies. It brings to mind a Faun's sublimation of love to 'Une sonore, calme, et monotone ligne.'[18]

In 'Purs Drames,' Valéry's first aubade, which is almost contemporary with three other of his early prose poems, we have seen the Valéryan prose poem come into its own.[19] But in its very newness and resplendent originality it yet reflects the sources which nourished it: on the one hand, the renewed vision and form of Rimbaud's *Illuminations*, and, on the other, and even more decisively, the Symbolist verse – and uni-verse – of Mallarmé.

In discussing this prose poem, I have frequently referred to Valéry's correspondence with Gide. The two young poets – it was Gide's period of André Walter – had been corresponding only since December 1890, and so these letters still belong to the ardent period of a correspondence whose main, indeed unique, theme is literature. The letters, moreover, are not merely about literature: some of them are themselves intended as *essais d'écriture*. In January 1890, Gide writes to Valéry about their correspondence:

> comme il me semble vous me le proposez, chacune de ces lettres serait quelque subtil paysage d'âme, plein de frissonnantes demiteintes et de délicates analogies s'éveillant comme des échos aux vibrations des harmoniques; – quelque spécieuse vision, que suivraient, doucement découlées, les déductions de nos rêves. Et ces sortes de confidences nous révéleraient bizarrement et délicieusement l'un à

l'autre, en apprenant à l'un comment chez l'autre s'associent ces
frêles images ... Dites-moi, je vous en prie, et bien vite – est-ce cela
que vous désirez – dites? ou si c'est autre chose? Toujours se pour-
rait-il que ces sortes de confidences ne soient qu'une partie de nos
lettres et le reste se pourrait remplir de quelque futilité plaisante – de
quelque récit *ad libitum*, de quelque songerie critique sur quelque
récente lecture – nous pourrions même, si vous m'en priez fort,
parler de littérature...[20]

When Gide, later in the letter, says 'Comprenez bien, je vous en prie,
que je ne classe point sous rubrique "littérature" nos propres productions et nos projets et nos rêves,' his very words, 'nos propres
productions et nos projets,' belie him. Both writers, moreover, are
deeply engaged in literary production; Gide has just published *Les
Cahiers d'André Walter*, and some of Valéry's poems, above all the
'Narcisse,' are beginning to attract critical attention.

The *écriture* of this correspondence, then, expresses not merely the
early stages of a friendship, but also the beginnings of two literary
careers. Valéry writes letters overflowing with lyric prose:

il y avait des artisans amis de la Mort qui lissaient avec je ne sais
quelle *éternelle* résignation, des pierres tombales, au déclin pâle
d'un beau jour d'hiver. La terre était maternelle et me faisait songer
à d'idéales, profondes, et solennelles fosses – des fosses d'âmes, au
déclin pâle d'un beau jour d'hiver...[21]

And Gide responds with equally exalted verse:

Mon âme sommeillait, ou peut-être en prière,
Voguait sur les lacs bleus de nocturne lumière
Car j'avais joint mes mains en geste de prière
Avant de m'endormir – afin de mieux prier.[22]

These samples are hardly typical, to say the least, of their authors'
characteristic manner, and when Valéry writes to Gide in March of
that year, 'Moi pour qui la poésie serait le suprême sacerdoce d'une
religion exquise,' we recognize in this stance Paul-Ambroise, the
young disciple of Mallarmé, and not the mature Valéry.[23]

I have dwelt on the epistolary background of 'Purs Drames' because
the prose poem grew directly out of it. For in one of these letters,
which contains also the germs of the early prose poem 'Pages Iné-

dites,' we find already a full development of the Symbolist garden, as well as one of the major images of 'Purs Drames':

> Venez donc réveiller les antiques roses et les lis penchés, comme un ange de jadis, un ange terrible et frêle, de jadis dont un souffle aurait de corolles suscité l'éveil rose dans des jardins, et qui des gestes de ses mains aurait fait obéissants les parfums pâles et les feuilles confuses, dans l'Eden?
>
> *Une étoile se posa sur un calice, et brille à travers la soie légére des pétales, et palpite. Ah! que de nuit! La saisir! La couver dans le creux des mains puériles et rire de la tenir captive, – une Etoile* [my italics].[24]

Thus, while reflecting the Symbolist background of Valéry's youth, and especially the influence of Mallarmé and Rimbaud, 'Purs Drames' already points to the mature prose poems and to one of their marked structural characteristics, which I have called 'the mobile fragment.' For here a fragment has moved from a 'poetic' correspondence into the *œuvre*, where it becomes, in almost unchanged form, one of the major symbols of a prose poem.[25]

3 Fragments

The prose aubades are essentially, I have said, mono-dialogues of the self with the self as it first discovers itself – its selves – and then its world upon awakening. The most minute, and at the same time most elementary, of Valéryan dialogues, the miniature, fragmentary 'Dialogue de Nuit,' from *Mauvaises Pensées et autres*, echoes this first moment of consciousness, of selves-consciousness:

> Qui est là?
> Moi!
> Qui, *Moi*?
> Toi.
> Et c'est le réveil. Le Toi et le Moi (o II, p 880).

At the very root of thought is that *dédoublement* which alone makes it possible: 'La pensée exige une division interne' (c I, p 1029), for thought depends on language, and 'penser est se parler' (c I, p 979); so that the individual mind is not single but double: 'L'individu est un dialogue' (c I, p 440). Valéry knew that 'psychology' and language are inextricably intertwined:

> Tout langage pose ou suppose Deux membres ... il y a deux persònnes en Moi – en *un* Moi – ; on *dirait* aussi: Un *Moi* est ce qui est en *deux Personnes* – mais ce sont *deux fonctions* dont *l'indivisibilité fait un Moi* (c I, p 467).[1]

II

Another fragment, 'Réveil,' from *Mélange de prose et de poésie*, reflects the exuberance of the fresh, awakening mind as it is overwhelmed by the almost simultaneous illuminations of ideas in its vast plain:

> Au réveil: trois, quatre foyers d'idées s'allument en des points
> éloignés du champ de l'esprit.
> *On* ne sait où courir (o I, p 338).

This fragment and the instant it objectifies recalls 'Aurore' and the
excitement of those throngs of ideas – 'Maîtresses de l'âme' – that
arise with the awakening poet:

> Ne seras-tu pas de joie
> Ivre! à voir de l'ombre issus
> Cent mille soleils de soie
> Sur tes énigmes tissus? (o I, p 112)

Our text's emphasized *'on'* stresses a still impersonal self, one that is
pure virtuality, a self that is not yet fixed, not determined by the person and personality which it must later assume. This joy at the pureness of a self as yet unlimited by that individuality with its history
inherited from yesterday, becomes a constant theme of Valéry's aubades. In a late notation of the *Cahiers* (1944), the poet still expresses
the same excitement at this first privileged moment of a pure, impersonal *moi*:

> Réveil.
> Il n'est pas de phénomène plus excitant pour moi que le réveil.
> Rien ne *tend* à donner une idée plus extraordinaire de ... *tout*, que
> cette autogenèse – Ce commencement de ce qui fut – qui a, lui aussi,
> son commencement – *Ce qui est*, – et ceci n'est que choc, stupeur,
> contraste.
> Par là, se place un état d'équidifférence comme si ... il y eût un
> moment (*des plus fragiles*) pendant lequel on n'est pas encore *la per-
> sonne qu'on est*, et l'on *pourrait* r*edevenir une autre*! Une autre mé-
> moire se développerait. D'où, du fantastique – l'individu externe et
> demeurant, et tout le psychique substitué...! (c II, p 198)

III

While the two preceding fragments deal with the awakening of the
self, the following short piece from 'Poésie Perdue' of *Autres Rhumbs*
(1927) is about the awakening of the world:

Les oiseaux

Oiseaux premiers. Naissent enfin ces petits cris. Vie et pluralité vivante au plus haut des cieux!

Petits cris d'oiseaux, menus coups de ciseaux, petits bruits de ciseaux dans la paix! Mais quel silence à découdre! (o ii, p 657)

There are several other prose aubades in 'Poésie Perdue,' as well as the three-part sequence 'Matin,' and a longer prose poem, 'Oiseaux Chanteurs.' Valéry wrote several animal prose poems, most of which are about birds, for they, like the matutinal poet, sing the rise of dawn. What fascinates Valéry in the bird is its freedom of movement and, above all, its song: 'L'oiseau seul et l'homme ont le chant. ... Chant et mobilité, un peu moins étroitement ordonnés par la circonstance qu'ils ne le sont chez la plupart des vivants' (o ii, p 660).

The 'first birds' are as it were born anew – 'naissent' – each dawn with their cries, and their concert is made up of so many tiny voices that they are a 'living plurality' and life itself 'in the highest of skies.' The poet renders these little cries with the highly original sound-image of 'menus coups de ciseaux,' echoing 'oiseaux.' Nothing could depict these early morning voices more faithfully than the 'petits bruits de ciseaux,' a simile which is then beautifully extended to capture the transitional moment, 'quel silence à découdre!'

The bird becomes the very symbol of renewed life elsewhere in Valéry's poetry. In 'Anne,' as the night of loveless love turns into dawn, the bird of reconciliation begins its song which 'quells the dead':

Mais suave, de l'arbre extérieur, la palme
Vaporeuse remue au delà du remords,
Et dans le feu, parmi trois feuilles, l'oiseau calme
Commence le chant seul qui réprime les morts (o i, p 91)

and as the Jeune Parque meditates on death, the bird's 'infant cries' announcing spring and morning recall her back to life:

...L'oiseau perce de cris d'enfance
Inouis ... l'ombre même où se serre mon cœur (o i, p 103).

In the 'A B C' prose aubades, the poet's very soul soars high, like a bird, to meet the rising sun:

...L'âme s'abreuve à la source du temps, boit un peu de ténèbres,
un peu d'aurore, ... et s'enfuit sous forme d'oiseau jusqu'à la cime à
demi nue dont le roc perce, chair et or, le plein azur nocturne.

IV

In all the above fragments the poet welcomes the dawn which renews
him and his world. In a contrasting text from the 'Cahier B 1910,'
which Valéry first published in the twenties and again in 1930, an
anguished self whose wakefulness precedes daybreak refuses the new
beginning; its light appears 'darker than all night,' and 'l'esprit' falls
victim to the anguish whose defeat is its very *raison d'être*:

> L'angoisse – revanche des pensées inutiles et stationnaires, et des
> va-et-vient que j'ai tant méprisés.
>   Angoisse, mon véritable métier.

If Teste and his idol – 'je confesse que j'ai fait un idole de mon esprit,
mais je n'en ai pas trouvé d'autre' (o II, p 37) – constitute the exor-
cism of this anguish, we know that he is himself but a fragment:
'Teste ... est un personnage obtenu par le fractionnement d'un être
réel dont on extrairait les moments les plus intellectuels pour en
composer le tout de la vie d'un personnage imaginaire' (o II, p 1381);
he is but a fragment of a much richer self, whose suffering, whose
victories and whose defeats inspire that very mind which creates the
song. Light is imperceptible without darkness, and each sun rises out
of and presages the night.

> Et à la moindre lueur, je rebâtis la hauteur d'où je tomberai
> ensuite.
>   ...Le jour commence par une lumière plus obscure que toute
> nuit – je le ressens de mon lit même. Il commence dans ma tête par
> un calme laissant voir toutes pensées à travers un état pur, encore
> simples, assoupies, distincts: d'abord, résignation, lucidité, bien-
> être, comme dans un bain primitif. Le matin premier existe comme
> un uniforme son.

Throughout the text, the poet develops that play of opposites –
'hauteur-tomber,' 'jour-nuit,' 'lumière-obscure,' 'angoisse-
résignation,' 'rêve-veille,' – which characterizes the moment which
is both night and day, darkness and light, and which makes up the
tension of the fragment.

Man is condemned, like Sisyphus, to existence and his days, to emerge from the primeval waters – 'bain primitif' – and embryonic well-being into a painful and unwanted birth and awakening:

> Bientôt, tout ce que je n'ai pas fait et que je ne ferai jamais, se dresse et me retourne dans mes regrets sur ma couche. Cela est fort, tenace comme un rêve, et c'est clair comme la veille. Je sens terriblement le bête et le vrai de ces mouvements. Inutiles, véridiques, sont ces démonstrations fatigantes. Il faut se mettre debout et dehors, dissiper encore une heure dans les rues où s'ébranlent les ordures. Laisser même le supplice inachevé (o ii, pp 588-9 and c i, p 50).

Finally the narrator must physically escape the torture which he cannot conquer mentally. This fragment, then, reflects a moment of defeat, and the 'aube refusée' has found expression elsewhere in Valéry's poetry. It has inspired the poem 'A l'Aurore':

> J'ai vu se feindre tant de songes
> Sur mes ténèbres sans sommeil
> Que je range entre les mensonges
> Même la force du soleil,
>
> Et que je doute si j'accueille
> Par le dégoût, par le désir,
> Ce jour très jeune sur la feuille
> Dont l'or vierge se peut saisir (o i, p 159).

Here the persona remains torn between the alternatives of acceptance or refusal of the young day, 'unable to close his eyes to an inevitable beauty, yet bound to the suffering he bears in his heart.'[2] This poem is from the mid-thirties, as are the first drafts of 'L'Oiseau cruel,' a sonnet which also has for its subject the refusal of the morning:

> L'aube dans l'ombre ébauche le visage
> D'un jour très beau qui déjà ne m'est rien:
> Un jour de plus n'est qu'un vain paysage,
>
> Qu'est-ce qu'un jour sans le visage tien?
> Non! ... Vers la nuit mon âme retournée
> Refuse l'aube et la jeune journée (o i, p 158).

In this sonnet, as in the traditional *albe*, the lover rejects the rising day and its beauties which threaten to end the night of love. The same motif is taken up, moreover, in the 'Fragments du Narcisse,' whose lovers 'curse' the sun:

> Mais leurs esprits perdus courent ce labyrinthe
> Où s'égare celui qui maudit le soleil!
> ...
> Ils se sentent des pleurs défendre leurs ténèbres
> Plus chères à jamais que tous les feux du jour (o i, p 128)!

V

But most of the time the poet welcomes daybreak – 'et à la moindre lueur, je rebâtis la hauteur' – and its regenerative force. Yet, the moment remains ever equivocal in its enchantment and at the same time sadness, in its 'lucidité presque douloureuse,' which we find in the following fragment of the 'Lettre (du temps de Charmes),' which Valéry published several times, as well as in many of the prose aubades dispersed throughout the *oeuvre*.

> Je descendais le matin dans ce parc, avant l'aurore. J'allais pieds nus dans l'herbe glacée. Le tout premier moment du jour exerce sur mes nerfs une puissance singulière. Il s'y mêle de la tristesse, de l'enchantement, de l'émotion et une sorte de lucidité presque douloureuse. A peine se colorait le ciel, je rentrais assez ivre de fraicheur et de volonté.
>
> Tu ne peux imaginer quelles matinées j'ai passées pendant ces deux ou trois mois d'été, dans cette riche région où le grand arbre pousse comme l'herbe, où l'herbe est d'une force et d'une facilité incroyables, où la puissance végétale est inépuisable (o i, p 1645).

The letter, dated 1918, is from that summer of the last war year which Valéry had spent with M. Lebey on l'Isle-Manière in the Channel.[3] It is the time of imminent victory, and for the poet one of the most fruitful periods of his productive life. In 1917 'La Jeune Parque' had appeared and magnificently marked Valéry's return to poetry, while almost immediately distinguishing him as the greatest French poet of his time. After the patient and passionate years of hard work on his major poem, all the 'Charmes' burst forth with something like the 'force et d'une facilité incroyables' of the vegetative growth depicted in our fragment. From the 1926 edition on, *Charmes* opens with 'Aurore.'

The fragment reflects some of the poet's latent strength and renewed vitality, which are in harmony with those of the morning garden he goes out to greet. For a privileged moment – 'le tout premier moment du jour' – there seems to be no distance between the self and the world, that luxurious edenic nature pulsating with life's inexhaustible energy. But as the line of dawn barely colours the early sky, the poet's enchantment is tinged with sadness, his lucidity touched by pain: Lucifer, the brightest of morning stars, will be extinguished by the very sunrise which it announces.

VI

A similar feeling of vital force and almost animal strength emanates from another text from 'Propos me concernant,' in whose preface Valéry explains:[4]

> Le texte de ces "Propos" assemble quelques notes et fragments prélevés sans ordre ni système dans une quantité de cahiers où il est question de bien d'autres choses que de l'Auteur en personne. Peut-être est-ce dans ce reste que son *moi* le plus nettement se dessine?
> Ce ne sont ici que des moments saisis et fixés tels quels, ça et là, au cours d'une quarantaine d'années...(o II, pp 1505-6).

One of these 'moments' where Valéry's '*moi* le plus nettement se dessine' is again reflected in a dawn fragment:

> Il est des instants (vers l'aube) où mon esprit (ce personnage très important et capricieux) se sent cet appétit essentiel et universel qu'il oppose au Tout comme un tigre à un troupeau; mais aussi une sorte de malaise: celui de ne savoir à quoi s'en prendre et quelle proie particulière saisir et attaquer. Chaque objet particulier lui paraît devoir diminuer, s'il s'y attache, la sensation divine de son groupe de puissances éveillé, et il pressent dans tout le jour qui va suivre une incarnation, et donc une réduction de cette illusion de pouvoir a l'état pur; que mon sens intime place au-dessus de tout...(o II, p 1532).

The aubade recalls the second fragment discussed in this chapter, where the refreshed morning mind does not know which of the many ideas lighting up within it to attack first. In the present text, which summarizes many dawns – 'il est des moments vers l'aube' – the protagonist is again 'mon esprit ce personnage très important,' objectified by the first-person narrator in the familiar *dédoublement* which permits him to observe his own mental 'fonctionnement.' As he compares his 'esprit,' in its hunger to take possession of the world, to a tiger about to attack a herd, the simile reduces the whole world, the 'Tout,' to the mind's passive prey. In its 'sensation divine de son groupe de puissances éveillé,' the self feels that the world offers it no resistance; it is virtually its victim, and the all-powerful, divine *moi* is solitary like a god. It is, then, paradoxically separated from the world which it owns.

But again the mind's divine instant is equivocal in its very transience, like dawn itself, which is already coloured by the day which will absorb it. Even at its privileged moment the *moi*'s divine, that is immortal, power is but an illusion – 'il pressent dans tout le jour qui va suivre ... une réduction de cette illusion de pouvoir à l'état pur' – like that of the 'aurore' which merely suggests in their sheer virtuality those forms that the rising day will reduce to their concrete and fixed limitations, their 'incarnation' and thus mortality. Did not God himself 'dissipate' his divine 'Principle' in the creation and realization of the world and its mutable and mortal forms?:

> Dieu lui-même a rompu l'obstacle
> De sa parfaite éternité;
> Il se fit Celui qui dissipe
> En conséquences, son Principe,
> En étoiles, son Unité.
>
> Cieux, son erreur! Temps, sa ruine ('Ebauche d'un serpent,' o I, p 139).

But this is, of course, Lucifer, 'MOI ... Des astres le plus superbe,' speaking. The mental 'pouvoir à l'état pur,' that of a silent Teste, which the poet's most intimate self places 'au-dessus de tout' is power unrealized, not in fact, but in pure potentiality – that of the tiger before the attack.

VII

One of Valéry's most accomplished aubades is the prose fragment 'Laure,' (o II, pp 857-8), which first appeared in *D'Ariane á Zoé: Alphabet galant et sentimental* in 1930, and then again as the centre piece of 'Trois Portraits' in *La Nouvelle Revue Française* in 1931.[5] The title, rich in multiple connotations, evokes an autobiographical figure as well as one of Western, and specifically Italian, poetic tradition, while at the same time constituting a phonetic echo of both the moment the prose poem objectifies, 'l'aurore,' and one of its two dominant colours, 'l'or.' 'Laure' moreover recalls the 'laurier' dedicated to Apollo, whose leaves traditionally crowned the poet laureate, and Valéry was probably the last to function in that capacity for his country in modern times.

Laura de Grassi, Valéry's maternal aunt, had died in 1848 of cholera at the age of sixteen, so that the poet knew her only in absence and as a memory venerated in the Grassi family.[6] Laura had died almost exactly five hundred years after the death of Laure de Noves, Petrarch's inspiration, who became her poet's Muse after her death (6 April 1348) much more than she had ever been in life. Valéry certainly associated the two Italian women, melancholy and *tristes* inspirations of poetry, in his mind, linking them to their prototype, Dante's immortal Beatrice. In two passages of the 'Eros' section of the *Cahiers*, the poet joins the names of Beatrice, which was also that of a woman he had loved, with that of Laure, the ethereal muse: '*Seul et seule font Un* – être seul à deux. Laure – *Béatrice*' (c II, p 431); in the other notation Valéry reflects on the mediaeval origin of love as inspiration of art: 'L'amour comme création artistique est dû au moyen âge qui d'une part l'a revêtu d'une espèce de sainteté (Laure, Béatrice) – et de l'autre l'a paré de la sombre couleur du péché' (c II, p 459).

Our two-part fragment is divided into four segments, the first of which, its opening sentence, is the poem's prologue; the second, the long paragraph of the first part, furnishes the (stage) setting, or frame, for Laura's entrée, which makes up the third and central paragraph; the last one is the poem's dénouement, its 'falling off' as it were. This fragment, then, is carefully structured and built around the figure which it celebrates. 'Laure' is a precursor of Valéry's meticulously structured prose sequences, whose sometimes mobile fragments are assembled like building blocks to form an architecturally harmonious configuration or form.

The poem's brief and tightly condensed opening introduces its dramatis personae, 'Laure ... avec moi,' its moment or time, 'dès l'aube,' and its space and *lieu*, 'dans une sphère unique au monde.' It identifies itself as an aubade, the first among those I have discussed in which the self is not alone but appears to admit another presence into its privileged space and time. 'Laure' and 'l'aube' not merely echo but suggest the second term's synonym, 'l'aurore,' thus further tightening the cohesion of the concise sentence. Its predominant /o/ sounds – the open /o/ of 'Laure,' the closed /o/ of 'l'aube,' repeated with 'au,' and the nasal /o/ of 'monde' – as well as its semantic and syntactic concentration evoke the figure of the sphere signified by its conclusion: the tightly drawn construct and circle of 'une sphère unique au monde,' in which the *moi* and 'Laure' and 'l'aube' are enclosed. In this aubade, then, the self, no longer alone, does not open out toward the world revealed by dawn, but, on the contrary, rather encloses itself, shuts itself and 'Laure' off in isolation from the outside, 'le monde.'

We encounter the 'sphère unique au monde' elsewhere in Valéry's prose poetry; in the prose poem 'Agathe,' one of whose alternate titles had been 'Manuscrit trouvé dans une cervelle,' the persona explores her mind and its transformations during a fragment of a night, and '[sa] sphère singuliére,' 'ce clos unique' (o II, p 1390) emerges as a figure for that mind, while on the physical level evoking the 'cerveau' alluded to in the alternate title.[7] Our poem's 'sphère unique' similarly symbolizes the awakening mind itself, 'cette forme fermée où toutes choses sont vivantes.' And the persona's room, 'les murs de ma chambre me semblent les parois d'une construction de ma volonté,' becomes but an extension of that mind. 'Le pur feuillet qui est devant moi' is Narcissus's mirror; Laura's apparition will be reflected in it: our poem, 'Laure,' written on the page.

I have said that in this aubade the persona is not alone, and yet his solitude is everywhere stressed: 'J'appelle *Solitude* cette forme fermée...' 'Pour que Laure paraisse, il faut que ... je sois idéalement seul.' That other presence which requires this '*Solitude* ... fermée' in order to appear is but a secret, and usually hidden, aspect of the *moi* itself; 'Laure' is the personification of its anima, 'âme,' which sometimes visits the mind at moments of its supreme attention and 'attente.' The mysterious feminine presence is the soul, which comes to share the mind's ideal solitude; it is an aspect of the self which is, in turn, a pure 'regard,' a glance whose 'puissance précise' and 'profonde fixité' pierce and penetrate the introspective mind.

The soul is present in other aubades, but only in 'Laure' is it personified as and identified with the virginal and inaccessible Laura. In some dawn pieces, the union of 'esprit' and 'âme' is threatened by the approaching day:

> Il est temps que vienne le jour avec son epée qui divise l'esprit de l'âme et découpe *aujourd'hui*...(c II, p 1290).

and in a dawn fragment from the period of 'Laure,' the poet addresses his soul as a rising morning star:

> C'est au réveil, au matin que l'*âme* se sent étrange – entre passé et
> avenir.
>   Elle se lève comme un astre – ...
>   Peut-être, n'es-tu que cet instant, cet effet, cette illusion de Moi
> pur, et la tristesse énorme d'exister – ... Tu ne viendras pas à bout de
> tout ce que tu éclaires, Ame. Toute ta prostitution diurne aux choses
> et aux actes ne peut rien contre ta terrible virginité – ... Miroir (c II, p
> 1295).

While Valéry the analyst condemns such terms as 'soul' or 'love' as
termes imprécis – 'me suis interdit d'employer aucun mot que je n'y
puisse attacher un sens *fini* – conscient – Jamais user de ce qui trouve
dans la pénombre du langage des résonances, des relais indistincts.
Le mot *âme* proscrit. Etc.' (c I, p 114) – these same words reawaken
infinitely enriched in his poetry and especially in his morning songs.

The first part of 'Laure' is a careful preparation for the secret meeting of animus and anima 'à cette heure première que je ne place ni
dans mes jours ni dans mes nuits.' It is a moment of pure expectation;
for Valéry love is most intense in its 'attente,' be it that of the beloved,
the 'Idée maîtresse,' or his muse:

> Ne hâte pas cet acte tendre,
>   ...
> Car j'ai vécu de vous attendre ('Les Pas,' o I, p 121)

This 'attente' and imminence, the moment of pure expectation, characterizes Valéry's aubades; its heightened intensity is celebrated
again and again, as dawn follows dawn:

> Est-il espoir plus pur, plus délié du monde, affranchi de moi-
> même – et toutefois possession plus entière – que je n'en trouve
> avant le jour, dans un moment premier de proposition et d'unité de
> mes forces, quand le seul désir de l'esprit, qui en précède toutes les
> pensées particulières, semble préférer de les surprendre et
> d'être amour de ce qui aime?
>   L'âme jouit de sa lumière sans objets. (o I, p 351)

In our poem's centre, in the persona's solitude and 'ce silence tout
armé d'attentes,' Laura's presence is manifest as an all-seeing glance
as bright as the sun – 'Laure-l'or' – so that the mind's eye can hardly
bear it, but which it cannot escape. Not even the *moi*'s innermost
voice, the most obscure whisperings 'entre mon désir et mon dé-

mon,' can escape Laura's eyes, their 'puissance précise,' their 'pouvoir interrogateur.' As the poem moves to its conclusion, their bright, burning intensity fades like the star in the morning sky. The most spiritual of senses, sight, is replaced by the most sensual, the olfactory – 'odoratus impedit cogitationem' Valéry quotes Saint Bernard in the prose poem 'La Chambre hantée' (o i, p 308) – and Laura's eyes fade away as the perfume of her dresses, her hands, and her hair rises out of the 'néant,' a past long dead. In the poem's – and dawn's – dénouement, Laura's intense spiritual presence is reduced to the recollection of 'la Laure qui fut de chair,' and her blinding glance to a fragrance lingering in the mind and in the room, 'le parfum trop délicieux des anciennes robes de Laure,' as the morning poem turns into one of mourning of 'la véritable Laure.'[8]

As Laura's fragrance evokes the smell of dead leaves burned in late autumn days, the poet evokes the traditional analogy between the dying year and human mortality.[9] Our poem, encompassing both birth and death, dawn and fall, suggests again the dialectic of darkness and light which makes up the tension of the aubades, and of the moment of dawn itself.

Though M. Teste scorns emotions such as sadness – 'considérer ses émotions comme sottises ... quelque chose en moi se révolte contre la puissance inventive de l'âme sur l'esprit' (o ii, p 70) – and though Valéry himself in 'Propos me concernant' says 'quoi de plus sot que la tristesse?' (o ii, p 1523), in his poetry, and especially the aubades, 'l'âme' frequently takes its revenge. For even that intellectual 'ivresse' and exultation of 'lucidité' characteristic of the dawn poems is a powerful emotion, and in our fragment Laura's visit leaves the persona literally 'overwhelmed' by that other emotion we have encountered in the aubades, 'une tristesse magique,' into which he falls 'de tout [son] coeur.'[10]

4   The Trilogy 'A B C'

In 1925 Valéry published in *Commerce* the three prose poems 'A B C,'
indicating on the title-page: 'trois lettres extraites d'un alphabet à
paraître à la librairie du Sans Pareil.'[1] This 'alphabet' was never completed; a modified version of 'A' appears under 'Poèmes' in *Histoires
brisées* (O II, pp 461-2), and the prose poem 'C' was republished by the
poet in *Morceaux choisis* in 1930, under the title 'Comme le Temps est
calme.'[2] Though each one of the 'A B C' poems constitutes a self-contained whole, as their separate publication bears out, the underlying
unity of these fragments makes up the integrity of the sequence's tripartite configuration. For these pieces constitute a series of three dramas,
each one complete and characterized by the opposing forces of its inner
tension, but all sequentially related in the progressive development of a
single theme. In 'A' the mind finds its body upon awakening at dawn; in
'B' mind and body unite as the self arises to the new day; and in 'C' the
united self takes possession of the world, the morning unfolding before it.
   The first poem begins 'Au commencement,' like *Genesis*, and this
beginning implies also the vocative 'ô commencement,' invoking the
aleph and alpha of the world and the word as if by incantation. This
incantatory and prophetic, rather than narrative, tone of the opening
chord is accentuated by the future of the verb: 'Au commencement
sera le Sommeil.'[3]
   In the beginning is sleep and absence, and the predominance in this
opening of the maternal /m's/ evocative of the origin of both the individual and of the race – 'mère-mer' – as well as the round /o's/
suggestive of the womb and of feminine night, sound a vague remem-
brance of an embryonic past:[4]

> Au commencement sera le Sommeil. Animal profondément en-
> dormi; tiède et tranquille masse mystérieusement isolée.

As upon awakening of consciousness the self separates itself from the universal manifold and the 'I' emerges from the world – which it at the same time posits – that *moi* itself becomes divided into body and mind. And so the three basic Valéryan 'points cardinaux de connaissance' upon which reality is founded, and which he designates by the sign 'CEM' in the *Cahiers* – 'C E M le mon-corps, le mon-esprit, le mon-monde ce sont trois directions qui se dessinent toujours' (C I, p 1148) – these three points constitute themselves. That is, they are constituted by the language which they in turn create, as the world and the word are born simultaneously. It is no coincidence that our fragment's title is the first letter of the alphabet. The three 'cardinal points of orientation,' that is the divided self separated from the world, are the verb's 'I,' its 'thou,' and its third term in the mind's soliloquy, which is consciousness. But the internal monologue, the act of thinking, is again the familiar dialogue: 'penser c'est communiquer avec soi-même' (C I, p 440). In our fragment's opening it is the *moi*'s dialogue of *esprit* and *corps* as they arise in and with the world: 'je me réveille.'[5]

The awakening mind – 'mon esprit' – contemplates its still sleeping body – 'mon corps' – which has carried it through the archetypal waters of night and unconsciousness like an ark, and which preserves it:

> arche close de vie qui transportes vers le jour mon histoire et mes
> chances ... tu es ma permanence inexprimable ... ô ma forme
> fermée, je laisse toute pensée pour te contempler de tout mon cœur.

The Parque's consciousness awoke to contemplate her body – 'Arche toute secrète, et pourtant si prochaine' – similarly, and we find the same division of mind and body in Eupalinos's morning 'oraison,' his supplication to his body's perfect form to inspire him and his art: 'O mon corps ... Mon intelligence mieux inspirée ne cessera, cher corps, de vous appeler ... Mais ce corps et cet esprit ... il faut à présent qu'ils s'unissent dans une construction bien ordonnée' (O II, pp 99-100).

As the insular self of consciousness – self-consciousness – rises from the *Urelement*, its material form, its body, appears to it like an 'island of time ... detached from the enormous Time,' while our poem itself measures out its form and duration from the eternal flux:[6]

> Tu t'es fait une île de temps, tu es un temps qui s'est détaché de
> l'énorme Temps où ta durée ... subsiste et s'éternise...

The circular images of the closed arc, the island, and the 'forme fermée' evoke the feminine not merely as origin supportive of the birth motif, but also as an end, as object of desire. Like Narcissus bending over the image which he loves, our mind-persona embraces the form which gives him life and sustains him: 'Je me penche sur toi qui es moi'; and the waking lover of our aubade sings his sleeping beloved who holds him enchained:

> Il n'est pas de plus étrange, de plus pieuse pensée; il n'est pas de merveille plus proche. Mon amour devant toi est inépuisable ... Tu m'attends sans me connaître et je te fais défaut pour me désirer.

Nowhere is Valéry's love poetry more passionate than in this morning song:

> Je suis le hasard, la rupture et le signe! Je suis ton émanation et ton ange. Il n'y a qu'un abîme entre nous, qui ne sommes rien l'un sans l'autre. Ma vigueur en toi est éparse, mais en moi tout l'espoir de l'espoir.

In this ideal rape and hymen – and the sharp and viril /u's/ and /i's/ of 'rupture' and 'signe' accentuate its male aggressiveness – the mind will take possession of its body like an angel of light, like a flaming knight:

> J'apparaîtrai à mes membres comme un prodige, je chasserai l'impuissance de ma terre, j'occuperai mon empire jusqu'aux ongles, tes extrémités m'obéiront et nous entrerons hardiment dans le royaume de nos yeux.

We recall that Valéry has rendered this act of love in which the self comes into self-possession with the same vigorous eroticism in 'Aurore.'[7]

But before animating the beloved form, the mind wants to prolong the sweetness of anticipation, that state of being and non-being – 'Douceur d'être et de n'être pas' (o i, p 121) – wants to contemplate still the sleeping body and listen to the beating of its heart, behold its features and its absent eyes:

> Au travers de ce masque abandonné tu exhales le murmure de l'existence stationnaire. J'écoute ma fragilité, et ma stupidité est devant moi...

Come not yet back to life, 'ô repose encore, repose *moi*...' For here, as in the traditional *albe*, the lover laments the end of the night as he greets the day. But the sun is rising, and as the mind beholds with tenderness – 'ma tendresse anxieuse est sur toi' – its sleeping form

> cette Chose s'agite ... et il y a un appel, une amour, une demande sup-
> pliante, un babil isolés dans l'univers...

It is a gentle birth from an embryonic past into 'des essais de lumière,' and finally: 'le miracle, les corps solides ... mes projets et le Jour!'

'ʙ' begins with the self 'bouleversant les ombres'; now it is no longer a *moi* speaking, but a narrator beholding 'l'être' – a body and a mind united – emerge from the vague shrouds of bed and night:

> divisant, rejetant les flots du linceul vague, l'être enfin se défait de
> leur désordre tendre. La vertu d'être Soi le parcourt.

As 'connaître' passes into 'être,' and meditation into action, the in-timacy of the *moi*'s monologue is broken, and the self steps back now, out of itself as it were, to observe itself as an object or event, the phe-nomenon Man:[8]

> l'unité s'empare des membres, et de la nuque jusqu'aux pieds un
> événement se fait homme.

The characteristic *dédoublement*, that heightened state of conscious-ness which allows the self to behold itself objectively, is here no longer the mind beholding its body, as in 'ᴀ,' but the *moi* observing the 'fonc-tionnement' of the total self, its body and its own thinking. The Parque awakens saying 'je me voyais me voir' (o ɪ, p 97), and Teste goes to sleep murmuring 'je suis étant, et me voyant; me voyant me voir, et ainsi de suite' (o ɪɪ, p 25). This self-objectification is carried to its extreme point in the prose poem 'Sur la Place publique,' whose protagonist explains: 'je m'observe qui observe' (o ɪɪ, pp 688-9).

Only after the lucid awakening of the whole being – 'être Soi' – does the actual dialogue begin, the 'colloque dans un être' of body and mind: '*Debout*! crie tout mon corps, *il faut rompre avec l'im-possible*! ... Debout!' In another morning poem, 'Chant de l'idée maîtresse,' the master notion summons its 'être' into being with the same vigor: 'Allons! Debout! Surgis. Ecoute!/ ... Eveille-toi, brise tes chaines, sois' (o ɪ, p 357). And while that 'Chant' is a matutinal monologue, the Idea's supplication ('Moi qui t'appelle. Moi qui ne puis rien sans toi./Moi, l'Idée') to the body to sustain it, the morning exchange of *esprit et corps* has also become one of Valéry's formal Dialogues, the 'Colloque dans un être,' where, as in our prose poem, the mind calls its reticent body into life: 'Allons ... Sors de l'instant ... Compose tes puissances ... /Renais!' (o i, pp 360-1). And after the resistance of matter has been overcome by mind, the two selves become *one*self: '*Je* suis debout!'

Our fragment's persona, the whole person – like the poet who never tired of poetizing it – is filled with wonder at the miracle which renews itself each dawn, that autogenesis, the re-creation of the self:

> Le miracle d'être debout s'accomplit. Quoi de plus simple, quoi de plus inexplicable que ce prodige, Equilibre?

And so the self takes possession of space, time, and number – 'rejoins tes dessins dans l'espace ... pénètre, avec des pas que l'on peut compter, dans la sphère des lumières' – takes, that is, possession of the world of man. But in the very act of recreating his universe, of entering 'la sphère des lumières,' Man regrets the passing of the night – 'rendre la lumière/Suppose d'ombre une morne moitié' (Le Cimetière marin,' o i, p 148). The nostalgia for the origin ('je t'abandonne quelque temps, Douceur de n'être pas!'), its 'charme invincible,' and also its threats, 'effrayante impuissance inconnue,' make up the tension of the remainder of the 'B' fragment, the moment between night and day. For while the newly risen self rejects, throws off, the creatures of the underworld, that other side of itself, it does not forget them:

> A ce soir, jeux obscurs, monstres, scènes impures, et vous, vaines amours!

Every awakening is a return from that descent 'dans les ténèbres de toi,' 'tes abîmes' (o i, p 112). As dawn aroused Semirarmis, 'Existe! ... Sois enfin toi-même!', her Appollonian lover, 'l'Aurore,' summoned her to arise again from the world of the shades: 'Tire-toi de tes ombres,/Et débarasse-toi d'un désordre de drames/ ... les monstres de ton sang' (o i, p 91). The fullest development of the theme of the return from the underworld in Valéry's poetry is that of 'La Jeune Parque,' her struggle with the dark forces of the night, the monster, the 'cher serpent,' which both repulses and entices her, tempts her to descend ever deeper, before the final victory of dawn: 'Fuis-moi! du noir retour reprends le fil visqueux!/ ... Moi, je veille' (o ɪ, p 98).

How dare one, asks our fragment's *moi*, cross that perilous night: 'comment se peut-il que l'on ose s'endormir?' And in 'ʙ' the nocturnal voyage is again, as in 'ᴀ,' imaged as the crossing of a dangerous sea:

> O qui me dira comment au travers de l'inexistence ma personne tout entière s'est conservée, et quelle chose m'a porté inerte, plein de vie et chargé d'esprit, d'un bord à l'autre du néant?

In the 'Colloque dans un être,' the morning's new self looks back on the crossing of the night with the same wonderment: 'N'est-ce pas une merveille supérieure que de penser que l'on possède en soi de quoi disparaître à soi-même...? Tout s'efface à la fois. Est-ce beau? Quand le navire sombre, le ciel s'évanouit et la mer s'éva- pore...' (o ɪ, pp 365-6). And the same image of the great ship pushing steadily through the night of sleep has inspired Valéry's prose frag- ment 'Final':

> Comme le grand navire s'enfonce et sombre lentement gardant ses ressources, ses machines, ses lumières, ses instruments...
> Ainsi dans la nuit et dans le dessous de soi-même l'esprit descend au sommeil avec tous ses appareils et ses possibles.
> Le Sommeil est plus respectable que la mort (o ɪ, pp 354-5).

Our middle fragment concludes with the *moi* arisen and ready for the new day, but remembering its night.

The third piece, 'ᴄ,' opens out upon the world, like the window from which the persona is beholding it, and captures the transient moment between *aube* and *aurore*, death of night and birth of day, that fragment of time in its purity, calm, and imminence, which Valéry elsewhere salutes: 'O moment, diamant du temps' (o ɪ, p 351)! Our persona at the morning window figures the self on the threshold of the possible, and at that privileged moment, an ideal present, the world becomes a pure reflection in the self; as the universal self it thus becomes one with the universe, it becomes its consciousness, its con- science, and its witness:[9]

> Comme le temps est calme, et la jeune fin de la nuit délicieusement colorée! ... il fait pur, il fait vierge, il fait doux et divin.

It is the whole *moi*, both body and mind – and soul – which takes possession of the world:

> Les volets repoussés à droite et à gauche par un acte vif de nageur,
> je pénètre dans l'extase de l'espace.

The image of the swimmer and the 'je pénètre dans l'extase' suggest again the virile eroticism of 'Aurore,' while the mind's ideal rape – 'tes idéales rapines' – of the world is, as always in Valéry, that of the eye:

> Je vous salue, granduer offerte à tous les actes d'un regard...
> Quel événement pour l'esprit qu'une telle étendue!

This 'commencement de la parfaite transparence,' when *corps*, *esprit*, and *monde* fuse in an ideal imminence and purity, inspired 'Purs Drames,' whose persona we saw behold dawn rising from his window, as the first hour became the first day of the world.

As the persona of 'c' steps out on his balcony, it is with a feeling of adoration and 'une amour infinie' that he approaches 'les choses' which are coming to life like him, which impinge on his senses and construct themselves for and in his consciousness:

> Je voudrais vous bénir, ô toutes choses, si je savais!...

But Man has forgotten the language of worship and the supernatural of a former age, of his childhood as well as that of the race.

Like the *moi-esprit* of 'a,' who in awakening turned to his *moi-corps*, like the self of 'b,' who in arising to the day glanced back on the night from which it had emerged, like the very hour which surrounds him, so the hero of 'C' is composed of an inner tension of opposites which makes up his essence:

> Sur le balcon qui se propose au-dessus des feuilles, sur le seuil de la
> première heure et de tout ce qui est possible, je dors et je veille, je
> suis jour et nuit, j'offre longtemps une amour infinie, une crainte sans
> mesure. L'âme s'abreuve à la source du temps, boit un peu de
> ténèbres, un peu d'aurore, se sent femme endormie, ange fait de
> lumière, se recueille, s'attriste, et s'enfuit sous forme d'oiseau
> jusqu'à la cime à demi nue dont le roc perce, chair et or, le plein
> azur nocturne.

The familiar image of the bird, that of the peak, or isle, and the colours 'chair et or' constitute the tonality of many of Valéry's prose aubades and also of the *aurores* of some of his great lyric poems. Waking and sleeping, day and night, infinite love and fear without measure, make up the self whose soul drinks in this morning hour, a few shades, a little dawn. As the exultation of the beginning and of birth – 'ô commencement' – contains the nostalgia for a return to the source and non-being – 'douceur de n'être pas' – so the self, collected for future action but saddened by past weariness, is at once an angel of light and a woman sleeping, 'esprit' and 'âme,' *animus* and *anima*. It is this total and androgynous human soul, a universal self, which soars like a morning bird to meet and sing a world and life. And this song, which is the poem greeting the day, the aubade, arises new with every dawn:

> Mille fois, j'ai déjà ressenti l'Unique...
> Mille fois, plus de mille fois, ce dont l'essence est d'être unique ...
> Chaque aurore est première. L'idèe qui vient crée un homme nouveau.[10]

Valéry has sung the profound melancholy of this hour, as well as its joy, again and again, each time uniquely.

The ascending movement of the third part of our trilogy, the elevation of the self, induced by the images of the bird, the peak and the tree, is heightened to 'the most extreme point' as the persona beholds the sky: 'il subsiste très haut peu de fines étoiles à l'extrême de l'aigu.' And the words of the phrase by their sound-look, the repetition of hard consonants, sharp /i's/, and the final 'aigu,' suggest what they signify, the cold, piercing sharpness of the sparkling on high – an image and reflection of 'la première lucidité.' But these stars are dying, like the moon – 'la lune est ce fragment de glace fondante' – and the same image of the melting moon accentuates the life-death tension of other aubades.

The poem's matutinal *moi* partakes of the abundance of this hour of becoming, which contains both birth and dissolution, the initial and the final:

> Je sais trop (tout à coup) qu'un enfant aux cheveux gris contemple d'anciennes tristesses à demi mortes, à demi divinisées, dans cet objet céleste de substance étincelante et mourante, tendre et froide qui va se dissoudre insensiblement.

The 'gray-haired child,' like the moment of twilight, comprises both past and future, is a self both melancholy with reminiscence and exuberant with promise. Valéry once said: 'ce qui me frappe le plus dans la mémoire, ce n'est pas qu'elle redit le passé – c'est qu'elle alimente le présent' (c I, p 1221). Both the *moi* and its privileged moment are expanded in the contemplation of past sorrows, half dead, half deified, like the moon. Again, at this point of heightened consciousness, the self steps out of itself to observe its own *dédoublement* – 'comme si je n'étais point dans mon coeur' – and it beholds two selves: its youth and its old age meeting at this hour of dawn:

> Ma jeunesse jadis a langui et senti la montée des larmes, vers la même heure, et sous le même enchantement de la lune évanouissante. Ma jeunesse a vu ce même matin, et je me vois à côté de ma jeunesse...

The poet's reminiscence of the dawns of his youth and their tears recalls those of 'Purs Drames' and its transparent sadness. In recalling the past and presaging the future, our fragment reflects the *moi*'s total possession of the present and of the self, a self which has reached its extreme limit of pure lucidity, both cold and tender, as it contemplates and knows its mystery – life – without understanding. It is the moment of the Angel's tears.

After reaching its extreme point – 'l'extrême de l'aigu' – 'connaître,' like the 'être' which sustains it, must come back to itself, like old age to its childhood, and pure lucidity – 'lucidité sans objet' – to the *moi* which it cannot transcend. The circle always closes, like the uroboros which swallows its tail.[11]

Yet there arises in the self, as inexplicably as those tears, a yearning for transcendence, a yearning to surpass all possible experience and even knowledge; not to know, but to glorify and praise – 'je voudrais vous bénir, ô toutes choses, si je savais! ... ' Prayer, we said, is a vague memory of the past, come back perhaps with the child in the self and the innocence of the hour of dawn. Elsewhere in one of his morning fragments Valéry says:

> Petit matin, petit jour, heure, peut-être, de la plus forte présence des *hérédités*. ... Dieu n'est pas invraisemblable, à cette heure-ci. Le souvenir d'une création n'est pas très loin. Le Fiat lux est une chose toute simple et qu'on a vue et entendue (c II, p 1271).

The self is both child and man; how can the one pray without the
other listening?

> Divisé, comment prier? Comment prier quand un autre soi-même
> écouterait la prière? –

The orison rising from that mysterious part of the self – the soul –
which escapes understanding, to that which transcends it – 'énigme,
mystère' – must therefore be a prayer in 'tongues,' an unknown
language – 'il ne faut prier qu'en paroles inconnues' – mystery for
mystery. Valéry, like Mallarmé, also admired the liturgical language
of the Church, and the 'c' fragment closing the sequence concludes
with an exhortation in the tone of the *sursum corda* of the Mass:[12]

> Elevez ce qui est mystère en vous à ce qui est mystère en soi.

The poet's morning prayer is the aubade, the poem glorifying and
praising the new day and the new self: 'C'est la première oraison!'
  In my discussion of the 'A B C' poems as a sequence of three dramas, I
have traced in them a complex play of opposites – sleeping-waking,
absence-presence, *corps-esprit, être-connaître, moi-monde* – which
makes up the dramatic tension of each individual poem as well as of
the whole trilogy. All of these antitheses may be subsumed under the
general dialectic of darkness and light.[13] But as one element in this
antithetical movement passes into its opposite, it is not cancelled, but
fulfilled and preserved. For the notion of the world is meaningful only
in and for a mind, and *esprit* rises out of the body by which it must be
sustained – 'C E M.'
  And the privileged hour of dawn itself is also both one and tripartite – like the *moi*, and like our prose poem sequence – containing
the past and carrying the future. Like Saint Augustine's unique
present – *praesens de praeteritis, praesens de presentibus, praesens de
futuris* – the 'aube' *is* also both the night from which it rises, and the
day which it becomes. In a 'Matin' prose poem of Valéry's later years,
he says: 'du bleu frais peint sur or, or et nuit, or sur nuit. ... la nuit se
fait voir à la lumière, comme l'esprit au réveil fait voir la naissance,
l'inexistence ... à la première lucidité' (o I, p 355), and in a fragment
from 'Choses tues,'

> la conscience sort des ténèbres, en vit, s'en alimente, et enfin les
> régénère, et plus épaisses, par les questions mêmes qu'elle se
> pose, en vertu et en raison directe de sa lucidité (o II, p 497).

It is according to the same dialectic, then, that in the concluding and culminating fragment of our trilogy, where the self reaches its extreme wakefulness and lucidity – 'la première lucidité' – that lucidity is set off against the *moi*'s mystery – 'ce qui est mystère en vous' – a mystery which is not merely preserved at this moment of clarity and 'lumière,' but which is all the more profound for it.

In the aubades, as in this whole poetic universe, 'lumière' is a symbol for 'esprit,' and so each morning poem celebrates a twofold birth. The theme of light in Valéry's poetry has been brilliantly discussed by J.L. Faivre, who sees its origin in the poet's childhood.[14] But the sunlit *enfance* in the town surrounded by the sea inspired not merely the theme of 'lumière' in the Apollonian poet, but also that of the 'commencement.' And the close interrelationship of the two themes, in both the 'A B C' sequence and in Valéry's poetry in general, manifests itself in two of its beginnings: 'Au commencement sera le Soleil – Au commencement sera le Sommeil.' The themes of the origin and of light combine to form the aubades, the single largest group of Valéry's prose poems and fragments, for at each new dawn the awakening *moi* needs the world in order to exist – as the rising sun needs human consciousness to reflect it.

5 'Trois Réveils'

Since Valéry so frequently published his prose poems and fragments in sequences such as 'A B C,' some of the poet's prose texts were presented in the form of similar series after his death. Several of these 'posthumous sequences' combine *inédits*, poetic fragments from the *Cahiers*, and texts that were already published during Valéry's lifetime. 'Trois Réveils' is a posthumous sequence joining three prose aubades, the first of which dates from 1889, when Valéry was eighteen years old, and the other two, taken from the 1944 *Cahiers*, from the end of his life.[1] Thus, like the 'c' fragment of the 'A B C' sequence, it links the poet's youth and his old age. There is no indication, however, that this editorial ordering reflects the intention of the poet.

The first 'réveil,' entitled 'Nuit à la caserne' and signed '17 novembre 1889 au matin,' was written during the first days of Valéry's military service at Montpellier and represents the poetic expression of this new experience.[2] Valéry had written many poems that year and read widely. In September he had discovered *A Rebours*, a book which became, as I have mentioned, the young poet's 'livre de chevet,' revealing to him not merely the decadents and the poet he was later to choose as his *maître*, but a genre in which two great predecessors, Baudelaire and Mallarmé, had excelled: the prose poem. Des Esseintes treasured 'une anthologie du poème en prose' including Mallarmé's seven early prose poems, from 'Le Phénomène futur' to 'Un Spectacle interrompu,' which for him 'étaient les chefs-d'oeuvre de Mallarmé et comptaient également parmi les chefs-d'oeuvre du poème en prose.'[3] And we recall that Valéry wrote and dedicated to Huysmans one of his own earliest prose poems, 'Les Vieilles Ruelles,' in the same year in which he wrote the poem under discussion.

In 'Nuit à la caserne,' Valéry attempts, as he had in 'Les Vieilles Ruelles,' a certain realism and 'écriture artiste' reminiscent of the Goncourts, who had also been revealed to him by *A Rebours*. It is thus a descriptive piece, somewhat in the manner of Mallarmé's early prose poem 'La Pipe,' and lacks that fragmentary, instantaneous quality, as well as the intensity, of the later aubades. Moreover, the 'time' of 'Nuit à la caserne,' as the author indicates, is from ten o'clock at night until daybreak, so that only the last third of the prose poem is in fact about dawn. But what differentiates this early prose poem most significantly from the characteristic morning fragments is its persona's extroversive stance. Not merely does he concentrate his *regard* on 'outer' phenomena rather than those of his own mind, but this outer world does not appear as a composition of the poet's mind, like the world of 'Purs Drames,' written only a few years later; instead the narrator here 'objectively' registers the elements that make up his environment, which he renders thus in a more or less 'realistic' fashion.

'Nuit à la caserne,' like some of Valéry's other early prose poems, is also formally more traditional in its title, which states the 'subject' of the piece in the manner of 'Les Vieilles Ruelles' or 'Une Chambre conjecturale.'[4] Thus, in these early prose poems there is still a wider gap between *forme* and *fond* than in the later fragments, which are not so much 'about' anything, as they are themselves the direct verbal reflections – celebrations – of the moment they objectify.

The poem's title and elliptical opening statement fix its place and exact time, the definite article universalizing, and thus rendering even more oppressive, the *lieu* which confines the first-person narrator introduced in the second sentence. The first paragraph establishes the poem's *cadre* as well as the persona's frame of mind: his twofold imprisonment, in the stony, black courtyard and in his loathing, is accentuated by the repetition of the preposition 'dans.' 'J'erre dans mon dégoût' suggests 'égout' in line with 'la cour rugueuse et noire,' and later in the paragraph evoked with 'l'abreuvoir.' The 'je' is further confined by the very night whose 'immense splendeur,' while it occasions a simile stressing the contrast between the narrator's sordid prison and the beauty 'outside,' consoles him but little. 'La tablette de velours sombre où le bijoutier jette ses rivières de diamants' is opposed to 'd'importunes lanternes troubles sous les voûtes,' and 'rivières de diamants' further contrasts with 'l'éclair d'une bayonnette.' The 'lointains' of 'les roulements lointains de roues' again underlines the notion of confinement, picked up in the following sentence-paragraph by 'ce bruit *extérieur* me rejette *dans* la douleur de *l'emprisonnement parmi* la sottise, la brutalité, et les têtes carrées *sous* le képi' [my italics].[5]

So far I have concentrated on the *signifié*; an examination of the *signifiant*(s) of the text's opening passages reveals its refined 'écriture.' Almost all of the paragraphs of the piece open, like the first one, with brief, sometimes verbless, phrases which in their telegraphic terseness establish a tone of reportage conducive to realism: '10 heures.', 'Dans la chambre.', 'On ronfle.', 'Un froid agréable.', 'C'est le réveil.', 'Tumulte dans l'escalier.' The poem's second sentence is carefully balanced, literally situating the persona between the confining courtyard and the immense night; the unconsoled *moi*, constricted by his own unhappiness, is flanked by the two prepositional phrases, 'dans la cour...' and 'par l'immense splendeur...' From the third to the final sentence of the opening paragraph, all sentences begin with the indefinite article, 'Une nuit...', 'Un calme frais...,' 'Un filet d'eau...,' thus constituting an enumeration of the elements that make up the opening scene, in which the narrator appears to be a stranger as much as the reader.

Internal echoes of dark vowels and nasals in the text reflect the dark yard and the night: '*dans* la *cour*,' '*dans mon* dégoût,' '*con*sole,' 'im*mense* splen*deur*,' 've*lours sombre où* le bi*jou*tier,' '*troublé* ... *lan*ternes *troubles sous* les *voûtes*,' '*roul*ements de *roues*.' Light vowels suggest the sparkling of the stars on the background of the night sky and of the jewelry on the black velvet, '*i*mmense splendeur de la *nuit*,' '*bi*jou*tier* ... *ses ri*vières de *di*amants,' 'l'*é*clair d'*une bay*onnette,' 'un *filet* d'eau.' The 'jette' of the first paragraph is echoed by 'rejette' of the second, which spells out the theme of 'emprisonnement,' and in which 'dans la douleur' recalls the earlier 'dans mon dégoût.' The prepositional phrase 'parmi la sottise, la brutalité, et les têtes carrées sous le képi,' an enumeration of aesthetic dissonances, is appropriately rendered by an accumulation of sharp vowels and hard consonants.

In the third paragraph, where the narrator has returned to the barracks and gone to bed, his imprisonment literally reaches an almost suffocating constraint: '*dans* la chambre ... *entre* la capote et la couverture.' Confined inside, behind 'les croix noires des barreaux,' he is even more estranged from that environment, whose phenomena he records in the most impersonal and distant manner. This distance is achieved by the use of indefinite articles, or even the complete absence of articles: 'des voix ... chuchottent.' 'Baillements, tremblotement de la maigre lampe unique.' The individuals about him, whom the darkness renders even more anonymous, are referred to by the impersonal pro-

noun: 'On l'éteint.' 'On se remue en des draps.' 'On jure.' Some of
the sentences are verbless: 'Dans la Chambre. Sur une couchette, sans
drap...,' and in some the verbs are nominalized: 'tremblotement de la
lampe'; some are inverted: 'Des voix, au fond, chuchottent.' Again, a
network of alliteration and internal rhyme makes up the tightly-
woven texture of our text: '*Dans* la *chamb*re. Sur une *couchette* ... entre
la *capote* et la *couverture*. Des voix, *au fond, chuchottent*. Baille*ment*,
tremblotement de la *lampe* unique *pend*ue *au plafond*. ... *ce n'est plus qu'on
point bleu ... qui se balance ... rythmiquement*. Une cla*rté* ... *tremble* aux
étroites fenê*tres*. *Au plafond parfois* se *projettent* ... les *croix noires*
des *barreaux* et *toute l'image tourne sur les poutres...*'

As in the beginning 'les roulements lointains,' 'ce bruit extérieur,'
called to the imprisoned self from the 'outside,' so toward the end of
the night he is visited from the 'inside' as it were, by his memory. And
though he cannot savour the poetry in his mind, it occasions the
poem's most melodious line: '...des sonnets de Heredia, des vers de
Mallarmé.'

But they are submerged in another rhythm, the 'mystérieuse mesure' of the anonymous snoring roundabout, as inescapable as the
pervasive 'odeur lourde' which surrounds the waking narrator. It is
this paroxysm of confinement, now oppressing all the senses, which
finally provokes the liberation, as the persona goes out to meet the
dawn and our nocturne turns aubade.

The breathtaking excitement of approaching day is reflected in the
series of brief, taut sentences preliminary to the first, sudden flicker of
light toward the east, 'un clignotement d'oeil clair,' 'un cri de
lumière.' Metaphor and synesthesia celebrate the advent and event
of dawn, the sunrise greeted by the vigilant bugle call which tears the
silence and the night with its sharp notes. 'C'est le réveil,' and everything stirs to life in a passage abounding in verbs – 'des bras se
tordent ... un souffle de lueur entre ... pique ... allume' – and culminating in the turbulant agitation of feet and multiple confusion of
voices: 'Tumulte dans les escaliers.'

Water begins to flow, and the wind is rising, both night and poem
coming to an end as the persona turns toward the renewal and refresh-
ment of 'le vent salutaire du matin.' In its conclusion this early prose
poem thus already presages some of Valéry's great lyric poems of imprisonment and liberation. The Parque, escaping the deadly temptations of her night, goes out to greet the salutary breath of morning.

> L'être contre le vent, dans le plus vif de l'air,
> Recevant au visage un appel de la mer.

And the *moi* of the 'Cimetière Marin' saves himself from the entice-
ment of 'la pureté du Non-être' by resolutely turning toward life:

> Le vent se lève! ... Il faut tenter de vivre!

Nothing could more acutely illustrate the contrast between Valéry's
early prose poems and his mature prose aubades than the juxtaposition
of 'Nuit à la caserne' with the two late 'réveils' of our sequence. The
first of the two untitled pieces, dated 'janvier 1944,' is made up of two
principal parts or fragments, the second of which is reproduced, with
very minor punctuation variants, in the *Ego* section of the Robinson
edition.[6]

As in the characteristic Valéryan aubade, the self of this 'réveil' is
by, and with, himself; it is still before dawn, and the awakening *moi* is
separated and isolated from the world of this last hard occupation
winter by the walls of his chamber, the surrounding night, and by the
very hour of his wakefulness in the sleeping city. His glance, moreover, is turned inward. Inside his mind is the stage on which opposing
forces play and are momentarily interlocked in a precarious equilibrium.[7] The dramatic conflict between the mind's waking and its
sleep, between that which thinks and that which is thought – the
mind and its ideas – presents itself as suspense, as a balance of forces,
and this equipoise is reflected stylistically in the symmetrically balanced structure of the opening sentences:

> ...je ne sais si je suis plus éveillé qu'endormi ou plus endormi
> qu'éveillé?
>   Il y a conflit parfois entre *Ce qui pense* et qui veut ne plus penser,
> mais dormir, et *ce qui est pensé* et qui *veut* se développer – voir son
> avenir.
>   Il y a donc deux suites possibles à cet instant.

In the second paragraph, the persona returns to 'ce Cahier,' and the
text here becomes self-reflective, reminiscent of Gide's 'composition
en abyme,' for the morning fragment is about writing the fragment in
the morning *Cahier*: 'Il y a des matins ... qu'à mon réveil et retour
devant ce Cahier je ne me reconnais pas tout à fait.'

I noted in the introduction of this discussion that the *Cahiers* were
Narcissus' constant mirror for half a century. Are they not then – both
the Notebooks and the fragments taken from them – simply about
Valéry the man, writing his 'diary' for and to himself? On the contrary, I must insist that the protagonist of the aubades is a 'persona,' is

'the self of the fragment or poem,' for, as the Valéryan myth of Narcissus and the image of the fountain suggest, the introspective glance
objectified transforms a 'self' into image and object. The image of a self
reflected and retraced in the form of the written word is stylized by
the medium which transforms it.[8] This is an important Valéryan
notion: the poet repeatedly reminds us that such a stylizing process is
basic to any form of literature. Whether the 'writer' of a notebook or
journal addresses himself or others, or both, he *writes*, and 'on écrit
pour se rendre plus beau, plus aigu, plus puissant – on écrit pour se
recréer, pour choisir en soi – pour éliminer certaines choses de
soi – pour additionner ses meilleurs aspects – on écrit pour s'entendre, pour se trouver un écho flatteur, pour éliminer' (c II, p 1151).
The 'je' projected and reflected in the *Cahiers* is one to be read, and in
the aubades as elsewhere in the *œuvre*, Valéry thus creates a 'writer-
persona,' as he creates a 'reader-persona,' whose interaction produces
the living work.

As our persona greets his matutinal reflection, he encounters an
unfamiliar image of himself. While the self of the 'c' fragment of 'A B C'
beheld himself 'à côté de [sa] jeunesse,' in our aubade the *moi*
comes face to face with its old age and the 'dégradation' revealed by
other Notebook entries of that period.[9] The confrontation of the self
with its decline is both threatening and liberating, for as the body
becomes progressively more petrified – 'plus dur, plus pétré que nature' – in anticipation of its approaching death, the mind, in its greatest maturity, attains moments of a lucidity projecting the self beyond,
and as it were 'above,' the reality of the living things and thoughts
which have made up its world. From such a vantage point, the momentary commanding perspective of life seen from the solitary summit of its culmination, 'reality' sinks into insignificance, into the
inconsequential, in the Olympian vision of one already passing over
and out of life.

Valéry has objectified that vision in the last 'ébauche' of his *Faust*
(published the same year as this aubade), in the Solitary's mountain,
'un lieu très haut ... roches, neige, glaciers.'[10] As Faust ascends to this
'solitude essentielle, l'extrême de la raréfaction des êtres,' he finds
'personne d'abord; et puis, moins que personne. Pas un brin d'herbe... La nature terrestre, à bout de forces, s'arrête épuisée un peu
plus bas. Ce n'est plus ici que pierre, neige...' (o II, p 381). Approaching
the Solitary, the personification of pure Nothingness, Faust asks himself 'pourquoi suis-je monté jusqu'à ce point critique?' The Solitary,
like the lucid self of our aubade 'sans pitié pour toutes choses men-
tales,' ruthlessly breaks the idols of a lifetime and hurls their frag-

ments at Faust: 'A quoi te sert ton esprit? ... Le parfait n'a pas d'esprit. J'étais plus intelligent qu'il ne faut l'être pour adorer l'idole Esprit ... Oui, Ordure, le ciel et la mort ont rendu les hommes pensants plus stupides que mes porceaux' (o II, pp 385-7). And as the Solitary demolishes that other human pride, language, Faust despairs: 'Ici? ... Qu'y trouve-t-on, que de la glace et vous?' It is this same solitary mountain top of deadly lucidity which inspires the closing line of the first part of our fragment: 'Car, sache-le, la *marque du réel*, c'est *l'insignifiance absolue*.[11]

But the persona cannot remain in the irrespirably thin air of this exalted plane, and in the second part of these morning notes, he simply re-enters the life of another day, 'je me lève.' As he prepares 'ce café initial rituel,' he reflects with scientific detachment about the three possible causes of its effect on his organism, the paragraph stressing the double nature of the *moi*, its specific physical activity ('je vais faire ce café') on the one hand, and its general mental functioning on the other ('on peut faire ces trois hypothéses'). The familiar *dédoublement* – which actually creates three selves: the beholder, and its vision of a 'mon-corps,' as well as a 'mon-esprit' – is continued in the following sentence-paragraph:

> Donc je vais, et d'une part, je sens les Idées (très diverses) m'envahir, se disputer la vie, etc. ... etc. ... mais d'autre part je me perçois allant et agissant en plein automatisme et somnambulisme.

As is characteristic of Valéry's 'aurores,' this awakening self is 'invaded' by a throng of ideas fighting for their lives in his mind, 'mon-esprit,' while the 'mon-corps' integrates itself in 'mon-monde' – 'c E M le mon-corps, le mon-esprit, le mon-monde ce sont trois directions qui se dessinent toujours' – with the mechanical regularity of physical laws.

The *Leitmotif* of the reflected image – 'Je ne me reconnais pas tout à fait,' 'je me trouve plus dur,' 'je me vois vieillard,' 'je me perçois allant et agissant' – recurs in the penultimate paragraph which is itself a mirror, for its spontaneous alliterations – there is no *rature* in the original entry – and balanced rhythm, its internal echoes, reflect the signified. *Forme et fond* are inextricably interwoven in the text:

> Je me perçois mon propre fantôme, mon *revenant* regulier. Tout ce que je fais fut déjà fait. Tous mes pas et mes gestes peuvent se passer de moi, comme les actes insensibles et essentiels de la vie végétative *se passent de nous*.

The aubades are variations on a single theme, like the dawns they objectify, like the 're-venant regulier' who 'comes back' from that other world of absence and night with each new day. And as the *moi* is integrated into the flow of life, it becomes part of the general circuit of nature and its mechanism, suggested above with 'ma chimie,' 'la modification moléculaire de ma composition,' and 'reprise chrononomique.'

Paradoxically, the *moi*'s very 'lucidité' which permits it to perceive its 'nature mécanique' is itself part of the great mechanism. For it is this matutinal clearness of mind, rested and refreshed from the night's sleep, that usually leads it to the discovery of the unforeseen. Our aubade's concluding statement, with its momentary balance of opposing forces – 'l'habitude'/'l'imprévu' – carries and conveys the energy, the concentrated intensity, and tension of the privileged moment of dawn.

Thus even toward the end of Valéry's life, his aubades preserve their youthful freshness and force. The already quoted final 'réveil' of our sequence (c II, p 198), written a little over a year before the poet's death, again expresses the same wonder and excitement of yet another awakening, miraculous 'reprise chrononomique':

> Réveil. – Il n'est pas de phénomène plus excitant pour moi que le réveil.

For this first moment of coming into being, 'ce commencement,' the regular return of the self and its world, 'ce commencement de ce qui fut,' appears once more as an 'autogenesis.' Creation seems to originate within and out of the *moi*, independent of external influences, as both the universe and the language which defines it – '*tout*' – arise with the awakening self: 'Tout l'univers chancelle et tremble sur ma tige.' But by the very use of the scientific term 'autogenèse,' Valéry suggests the paradox of an endogenous creation of the world in a self *which is in the world*, or that of the formation of language in a *moi*, which finds and defines itself in language. Once more, then, the poet suggests the precarious equilibrium of a moment when the *moi* feels itself both creator and creature of '*ce qui est* – et ceci n'est que choc, stupeur, contraste.'

'Par là,' at this critical point, 'se place un état d'équidifférence comme si ... il y eût un moment (des plus fragiles) pendant lequel on n'est pas encore la *personne qu'on est*, et l'on *pourrait re-devenir une autre*!' At this 'fragile' point in time, the transient moment between night and day, the *moi* is in a state of equidistance between absence and presence, is a pure virtuality like the surrounding world, whose forms are coming into existence but are not yet imprisoned in it. Valéry frequently likened this 'Moi pur' – pure of those traits which will compose and fix and limit it – to the 'Zéro mathématique,' an ideal state of total absence and neutrality which is, however, of a virtuality without limits:

> La meilleure image du MOI est bien le Zéro, qui, d'une part, exprime le sans-attribut, ni image, ni valeur du "moi pur" qui s'obtient par exhaustion, puisque *tout* ce qui se propose à la conscience est un *Antégo* par là même; et d'autre part, le zéro multiplie par 10 le nombre donné – comme la perception qu'un fait quelconque nous intéresse en personne et doit être décrit en employant *moi, mon, me* etc. lui communique une valeur aussitôt incomparable...
>
> Ainsi, ce *qui se connaît comme rien en soi* est cependant un excitant de *valeur incomparable* (c II, p 327).

Because this ideal self, 'le Moi pur,' meets its privileged moment at dawn, it haunts the poet's aubades and many a morning note. In another *Cahier* of 1944, Valéry, then the most famous living poet of his language, says:

> Age, dégradation...
>
> Le nouveau, c'est que je me trouve par-ci par-là en présence du seigneur *Yo-Mismo* – Non de ce "moi pur," mon éternel agent – Mais d'un personnage *Moi* – Auteur de telles oeuvres, – situé, défini – donc le plus Antégo possible, car toute définition m'a toujours été insupportable...
>
> Or, je me trouve à présent un état civil et des attributs – toutes les impuretés possibles, tous ces produits de hasards...
>
> Je me dis, avec mon serpent, que l'être est un défaut dans la pureté du Non-être (c I, pp 222-3).

6   Three 'Matins'

The three morning prose poems to be discussed in this chapter, two sequences and one separate fragment, each entitled 'Matin,' were written in the twenties; all have their origins in the *Cahiers*.

I

The first three-part 'Matin' sequence (o ɪɪ, pp 658-9) was first published in 1926 in *La Revue de France*, where it bore the title 'Réveil' and was part of another, longer prose sequence, 'Rêves.'[1] Valéry then incorporated it, with variants in blocking and punctuation, into 'Poésie perdue' of *Autres Rhumbs*, which first appeared in 1927. It is this version which we are examining. Here the prose poem is entitled 'Matin,' its first fragment retaining the subtitle 'Réveil.' But part of the sequence (its first two fragments) had already been set down in a 1913 *Cahier* entry, under the title 'Réveil' (c ɪɪ, pp 1261-2). Thus 'Matin,' from which I quoted in the introduction, strikingly demonstrates the structural characteristic of the 'mobile fragment'; for here the poet added a paragraph (which was to become our poem's third part) to one *Cahier* fragment, inserting the two into the long prose sequence 'Rêves,' where they constitute the seventh and final section. Subsequently he removed this two-part 'Réveil' section from that sequence and divided it into the three fragments of the final 'Matin.'[2]

Like the jeweler, the poet, having cut the diamond, keeps it patiently in store – the vast storehouse of the *Cahiers* – for years, until the opportune moment, when he polishes and freely combines it with others in various settings to sell in the literary market-place.[3] But while the jeweler can only insert his precious stones into one mount-

ing at a time, the poet's fragments can sparkle in various settings or
sequences simultaneously.

'Réveil' opens with the opening of the eyes to dawn's illumination,

> Au réveil, si douce la lumière et beau ce bleu vivant![4]

the opening of the lips to a kiss,

> Le mot "Pur" ouvre mes lèvres,

and the salutation of the morning by the Adamic word:

> Tel est le nom que je te donne.

Each line is set off as a separate moment of consciousness which
gradually discovers and recovers its point in time, 'Ici...' The first sentence rhythmically reflects the event of awakening, 'au réveil,' the
pause of recognition marked by the comma, and then the gentle merg-
ing of perceiving with the perceived in an alexandrine whose caesura
divides it into two hemistiches, one of two symmetrical three-syllable
units, and the second of three rising iambic feet:

> si douce – la lumière – et beau ce bleu vivant!

At the same time this opening phrase, rising from 'réveil' to 'vivant,'
phonetically constitutes a combination of tones blending harmoniously through the juxtaposition of dark and light vowels /o/, /u/, /e/,
/y/, and /i/, as well as multiple alliterations, that of the r's (*réveil*
lumière), the l's (*la lumière bleu*), the labial fricative v's (*réveil*,
vivant), and the gentle labial b's (*beau*, *bleu*) with which the lips are
beginning to shape the kiss.

This 'matin,' which the poet names 'Pur,' recalls 'Purs Drames,' the
transposition of the same moment into a Symbolist poem some thirty
years before our aubade. Now both the traditional fable and its style
have been transcended, as the prose poem has evolved into the poetic
prose fragment. 'Pur,' simple and immaculate, are both the moment
before day, that fragment of time, and the poetic fragment, purified
now of any fabulation, which reflects it.

At this awakening, the poet's mind appears harmoniously integrated in the world, its 'perfect thoughts' linked to the day in one and

the same imminence. The absence of the verb 'être' in the present,
though it appears in both past and future tenses, stresses the virtuality
of both thoughts and day, the mind and the universe, neither as yet
limited by any particular reality, their being not in (f)act, but in
potentiality:

> Ici, unies au jour *qui jamais ne fut encore*, les parfaites pensées *qui jamais ne seront* [my italics].

Again the sentence's symmetrically balanced structure and rhythm,
reaching both backward and forward in time, as well as its internal
echoes, accentuate the perfect equilibrium of the moment and of the
moi in its world.[5] The poet then metamorphoses, and thus fixes, the
moment's essence, its virtuality and promise, into the metaphor of the
seed which contains a universe in germ: 'En germe, éternellement
germe, le plus haut degré universel d'existence et d'action.' Virtuality
is again suggested by the omission of the verb 'être,' while the paradox of the 'eternal seed' points to the fixing of the fleeting and transient into the permanent – if not eternal – by the poet: *ars longa*...
   'Le Tout est un germe – le Tout ressenti sans parties – ,' as the universe awakens, sketched in gold upon blue, 'et que nulle affection
particulière ne corrompt encore.' This universal unity and original
oneness before day's divisions again brings to mind 'Purs Drames,'
whose diverse images, 'corrumpues encore, par la certitude de leurs
éléments,' the poetic vision finally reduced to its essence, 'une ligne
sur l'espace céleste ou vitale.' The self, I have said, feels not yet separated from the All in and with which it is reborn: 'Je nais de toutes
parts, au loin de ce Même, en tout point où étincelle la lumière,'
the light which is everywhere:

   sur ce bord, sur ce pli, sur ce fil de ce fil
   dans ce bleu d'eau limpide.

'La lumière,' the 'Tout' in which everything rises to view, is, as I
have said, a symbol for the mind in this poetic universe, that human
consciousness without which the world would be devoid of meaning.
It is in this sense, then, that *corps, esprit,* and *monde* are born together.
The above 'au loin de ce Même' read 'au loin de ce Moi' in the *Cahier*
version, which pointed more explicitly to the *moi*'s integration in its
monde, adding: 'je suis analogue de ce qui est.'

In the conclusion, as in the opening, the persona apostrophizes the morning, the 'matin' pronounced for the first time in the fragment's last word. In this apostrophe, the poet turns away from the self and toward the morning world of which he is nevertheless an essential part, its consciousness. For a moment, then, the self is not self-reflective, but becomes the eye and voice reflecting the shapes and tones, the pure surfaces of a world emerging:

> un effet délicieux de lumière et de rumeur, merveille de feu, de soie, de vapeur et d'ardoise, ensemble de bruits simples confondus, dorure et murmures, matin.[6]

And as Valéry here approaches an almost three-dimensional celebration of colours and textures in praise of the sheer appearance of things, he at the same time realizes Baudelaire's dream of 'le miracle d'une prose poétique, musicale ... assez souple et assez heurtée pour s'adapter aux mouvements lyriques de l'âme.' The *Cahier* version had insisted, again more explicitly and thus less suggestively, on the musicality of both the moment and the poem: 'l'ensemble de feu, de soie, d'ardoise, de vapeur et de musique brute simultanée – .'

The 'Réveil' fragment of this 'Matin,' then, is the reciprocal reflection of the 'Moi pur' as it is born into a renewed world and the birth of that world in the *moi*. Its second section reflects the passing of daybreak into day, and day's first reduction – 'le jour avec son epée qui divise l'esprit de l'âme et découpe *aujourd'hui*' – of the Universal into the particular(s). The self hesitates on 'today's' threshold before entering its confining limits; it wishes to refuse the burden of a particular past and future, a personal history, as well as the constricting limitations of a specific person(ality). We find this regret repeatedly in Valéry's poetry, and especially in his prose poetry and the aubades, which are haunted by the ideal 'Moi pur,' the potentially powerful 'Moi-Zéro.' Elsewhere in the *Cahiers* Valéry says: 'Il y a quelque chose de terrible à être ce que l'on est. Si moi est quelque chose, il est rien. L'orgueil véritable est une résistance toute vivante, essentielle à l'individu' (c II, p 293). The second movement of our poem intones this nostalgia in a minor key; almost the entire section is made up of a series of rhetorical questions in the manner of the traditional *ubi sunt* complaint:

> Que ne puis-je retarder d'être moi, paresser dans l'état universel?
> Pourquoi ce matin me choisirais-je? Qu'est-ce qui m'oblige à reprendre mes biens et mes maux?

The longing for the pureness of a new beginning, personified here by the man who abandons his personal belongings on the seashore, had appeared already in the early (1898) prose fragment 'Agathe,' whose persona muses:

> A cette heure qui ne compte pas qu'importe toute mon histoire? Je la méprise comme un livre. Mais c'est ici l'occasion pure: défaire du souvenir l'ordre mortel, annuler mon expérience ... et par un simple songe nocturne, me déprendre tout à fait, y méconnaître ma propre forme (o II, p 1390).

Our poem's persona similarly finds in the present moment 'l'occasion pure':

> le matin, n'est-il le moment et le conseil impérieux de ne point res-sembler à soi-même? Le sommeil a brouillé le jeu, battu les cartes; et les songes ont tout mêlé, tout remis en question...

This 'Awakening,' then, is a reciprocal reflection of a twofold birth, that of the self in the world, and that of the world in the self; the second section ends: 'Au réveil il y a ... une naissance de toutes choses.'

The final fragment encompasses both sea and sun, female and male, 'âme' and 'esprit,' and so again demonstrates the close interrelationship of the themes of the origin and of light in the aubades:

> L'âme boit aux sources une gorgée de liberté et de *commencement*
> *sans conditions*...
> Ce Soleil qui paraît ... il s'annonce et monte comme un juge.

As the god-like sun, 'rising like a judge' from the maternal horizon of water and earth, begins its trajectory toward the high stillpoint of noon – 'midi le juste' – it convokes that land and water to a festive salute. It summons vague night-thoughts – 'les monstres de ton sang' – to the tribunal of Pure Reason, in a passage abounding in legal terms: dreams will be condemned, terror's judgments will be broken, and the mind's errors in procedure nullified. The spirit is illuminated and matter fecundated by the Apollonian god.

II

Our second 'Matin' (o II, p 661), a separate fragment, dates from 1927, when Valéry published it in 'Poésie perdue' of *Autres Rhumbs*.[7] This, like the preceding piece, had also been ready, with some variants, in the form of a 1921 *Cahier* entry, awaiting its time and place to appear.

This aubade reflects, again, the outer morning world – its sky, and sea, and land – rather than the inner phenomenon of the mind's awakening. It is, in fact, a fragment of multiple mirror reflections. The matutinal eye mirrors – and 'toute ma peau' feels – the 'pluie d'une aurore mêlée,' the world in which sea and land, in turn, reflect the sky's changing moods: 'Par le moyen des nues, le caprice du vent change en deux ou trois minutes la face du champ de la mer.' Here the metaphor of the 'face of the ocean's field' combines both land and sea and the notion of these as a beholding and reflecting eye. This big mirror of the sky and its rapid changes, water and land,

> une partie de la côte ... nette et sombre; l'autre toute fondue et vaguement écrasée dans l'humide substance de la vue,

then becomes itself reflective of a *paysage d'âme* and its fluctuating impressions from smile to sadness:

> Tout ce regard me peint les fluctuations, les invasions et désertions de l'âme par les lumières et les ombres des idées.

Finally, these rapid inner mutations, which are reflected in the outer ones – where they are rendered visible in the morning sky and its swiftly driven clouds, which are in turn mirrored in the tones and textures of sea and land – could well be reflected in a musical development, that is in art:

> La vitesse de ces changements *visibles* est de l'ordre de grandeur de celle de l'âme. Le mouvement d'un développement musical pourrait suivre celle-ci très exactement [my italics].

Throughout the fragment, the poet stresses *seeing* ('je regarde...,' 'c'est ma peau qui voit,' 'tout ce regard me peint...,' 'ces changement visibles...'), for the dominant mode of perception is again 'avant toute chose, celle de *voir*.'

At the same time, the rain and the sea, 'cette pluie rapide,' the 'champ de la mer,' the landscape which is 'la côte,' and finally 'l'humide substance de la vue,' relate this aubade to the second largest group of Valéry's prose poems, those celebrating the sea. This is further suggested by the sole other notation on the original *Cahier* page, which reads: 'La mer, la plus intacte et ancienne chose du globe. Tout

ce qu'elle touche est ruine; tout ce qu'elle abandonne est nouveauté.'[8]
What is once more apparent in the juxtaposition on the same page of
these entries – the one a dawn, the other a marine fragment – is the
close interrelationship of the themes of light and of the beginning,
not merely in the aubades themselves, but in this entire poetic universe. Its creator, while speaking of his 'Inspirations,' once said: 'Je
m'accuse ... d'avoir connu une véritable folie de lumière, combinée
avec la folie de l'eau' (o I, p 1090).[9]

III

The third 'Matin' (o I, pp 355-6), a two-part sequence, also originated
in the 1921 *Cahier* (c II, pp 1272-3), where it still shows some of the
poet's hesitations in the choice of certain words, as well as certain
variants in punctuation and blocking. The final version did not
appear until 1939, when Valéry placed it in 'Poésie brute' of
Melange.[10] This 'Mixture,' according to its author's 'Avis,' is 'une sorte
d'album que j'ai formé naguère de fragments très divers' (o I, pp
285-6); for, as he continues in the little opening poem,

> MELANGE C'EST L'ESPRIT
> Ce qui vint du sommeil, ce qui vint des amours,
> Ce que donnent les dieux comme des circonstances
> S'assemble en cet Album de fragments de mes jours.

'Poésie brute,' which also includes free verse like the beautiful morning poem 'Chant de l'idée maîtresse,' as well as the matutinal prose
sequence 'Méditation avant pensée,' moreover constitutes one of
Valéry's own definitions of the poetic prose fragment. And the ideal
setting for this 'poetry in the rough' is precisely 'ce mélange/Duquel,
à chaque instant, se démêle le MOI.' In all of Valéry's poetry, it is in
the poetic morning fragments, the prose aubades, that we most intimately witness this *Moi* 'disengage itself,' each dawn anew, out of the
'mélange' of the mind.

'Matin' opens with a general statement about a specific personal
self: 'Rien ne *me* touche plus que *le* matin de l'été,' echoing 'il n'est
pas de phénomène pour moi plus excitant que le réveil.' Again, as
we proceed into the unique dawn of this particular aubade, '*cette*
paix...,' '*cette* pudeur...' the poem's *moi* becomes impersonal, '*on*
dirait...,' '*on* sent...,' '*on* salue...' This shift shows again both the familiar splitting and distancing of the self from the self, as well as its

pureness, or freedom from personal traits: 'on n'est pas encore la personne qu'on est.'

As dawn's first lines appear upon the summer night, night, paradoxically, appears painted against dawn, 'cette paix du bleu frais peinte sur or,' in the poem which captures – black on white – the precarious moment balancing the antithetical forces of night and day: 'on dirait que la nuit se fait voir à la lumière.' Day against night, night against day – 'or et nuit, or sur nuit' – reflect the universal dialectic of light and darkness, of being – 'la naissance' – and nothingness – 'l'inexistence' – the very duality of Man, *homo duplex*. And this dialectic underlies the whole poem.

The central sentence of the second paragraph constitutes an equation which explicitly states the equivalence of 'lumière' and 'lucidité,' or, as we have said, light as symbolic of the mind:

> Il y a un instant où l'on dirait que la nuit se fait voir à la lumière, comme l'esprit au réveil fait voir la naissance, l'inexistence, et les rêves, à la première lucidité.

At the same time, in this equation the paradoxical inversion – in which it is not light that is seen in the dark but, conversely, night that becomes visible in the light – is extended to the right side, or second segment, of the figure: it is the mind's non-existence that becomes exposed in its first lucidity. What the text insists on – as does the very form of the equation itself – is the basically binary nature of the phenomena of perception, that is the binary structure of the perceiving mind, as well as that of its language. Light is meaningful only against the night, 'réveil' against 'sommeil,' in both the mind and the language which are inextricably intertwined in the psyche and in the logos, the psychology, which, since the Greeks, has been the controlling principle of the human universe.[11]

But the philosophical import, the 'meaning' of the text, is at the same time dressed in the stuff which makes it a poetic texture. For poetry itself – be it verse or prose – rests, as Valéry frequently reminds us, on the harmonious fusion of an underlying duality, that of *forme* and *fond*:

> La poésie (art) est un discours marqué par la valeur comparable et continue du son et du sens – par l'art de faire concourir au même objet ces excitations très différentes.

> Il en résulterait une définition de ce même objet – qui est ce qui
> peut être aussi bien créé et accru par ces deux moyens à condition
> qu'ils soient employés simultanément (c II, p 1114).

The second paragraph's vocabulary cluster, its synesthesias and
tropes which render the abstract concrete, visible, and palpable,
confer on its underlying thought a tonality which poetizes the
moment, for tender is the night, as is this dawn:

> Nudité de la nuit pas encore bien habillée. La substance du ciel est
> d'une tendresse étrange.

The new world appears child-like in its modesty and naked still, like
the night, as it emerges in and by means of the sun which draws forth
a universal birth, the birth of the universe – 'la naissance de toutes
choses.' The moment is felt as a present pregnant with the future: 'On
sent jusqu'à l'intime cette fraicheur divine, qui sera chaleur tout à
l'heure.'

While the first paragraph of the fragment concentrated on the
monde, the second centres around the *esprit* which, like the world,
is divided between antithetical forces: 'lassitude-travail,' 'tristesse-
espoir,' 'promesse-vanité de la promesse.' These opposing tendencies
of the mind again suggest an analogy with art, this time painting, in
harmony with the poem's tone – 'cette paix du bleu frais peinte sur
or' – for all of these moods appear simultaneously, 'peint comme un
tableau naïf où les actes divers d'un personnage sont rapprochés,'
against dawn's blue background of 'calme et pureté.' The self, like
the world, is new-born, but yet older by another day, full of potential
power, but hesitating on the threshold between passivity and action.
Lassitude, melancholy weariness, and even despair are characteristic
of the moment which, we found, is almost always equivocal in its
concurrent enchantment and sadness, and these qualities mark it with
what Valéry elsewhere calls a 'lucidité douloureuse.' In our aubade,
the persona's despair is brought to consonance and harmony with the
calm and purity; and thus world and mind are rendered so transparent that his sadness becomes the 'tristesse dorée, et d'un dieu' which
lucidly sees 'toute la pauvre vie dans un cristal.' But (and this is the
miracle which the aubades celebrate) the eternally returning moment
is new, pure, naked, tender, and of a 'fraicheur divine,' like the primi-
tive painting, 'un tableau naïf,' and the self both virginal and wise,
divine and innocent, as it hesitates on the shore. The essence of both
the poem and the moment, the tension of its stammerings and its pro-

mise, supported throughout by the birth metaphor which itself culminates in the final image of the Annunciation, is contained in a figure tense with virtual energy, the

frisson préalable à la mer.

This ellipsis, which contains both symbol and metaphor – the sea standing for both day and life – harmonizes stylistically with the context of surrounding sentences, which all lack the finite verb, 'peur d'entrer dans le jour,' 'tristesse dorée, et d'un dieu,' 'désespoir paisible de ne plus croire,' 'avant toutes choses,' 'invocation muette à ce qui va être.'

'Avant toutes Choses' later became the title of another morning fragment; and many of these fragments are, like the present one, invocatory: 'invocation ... à ce qui va être.' As the self and the world are still close to the source – 'l'âme boit aux sources' – and to the origin, they are still in proximity with the divine. Valéry has called the morning poem 'la première oraison,' and in our 'Matin' we find a whole vocabulary cluster modulating this tonality – 'fraicheur divine,' 'tristesse d'un dieu,' 'invocation' – and leading up to the culminating 'salutation de l'ange qui annonce qu'on est fécondé, gros d'un jour nouveau.'

The final 'Partage' marks the divide between daybreak and day, as well as that between the two parts of the sequence. In its short second fragment we follow the body's groping return from inertia to alertness. And the bilateral form of that body – so secretly and intimately linked to the binary structure of its mind – is reflected in the stirrings which bring it back to life:

le corps s'étire, se tourne et se retourne, cherche une torsion et une tension qui lui fassent reconnaître sa place dans lui-même.

As body and mind – 'l'esprit aussi se feuillette' – have finally come together in a single readiness, and the persona enters the day, 'Dieu se cache peu à peu...'

7 'Reprise'

In 1927 Valéry published 'Reprise' (o II, pp 661-2), a sequence of two fragments, in 'Poésie perdue' of *Autres Rhumbs*, where it appears immediately after one of the 'Matins' which we have discussed.[1] 'Reprise' celebrates the renewal of three different worlds at dawn; in I, the vision sweeps over the sea and landscape unfolding gradually in the first morning light; then it contracts to concentrate on the poet's page itself, on which the poem, like the day outside, is being born. From the worktable we move, in II, to the workings of the creative mind itself; the entire second fragment is devoted to 'Esprit.'

The title, whose multiple connotations the poem will develop, suggests in the opening passage the 'repetition' of a musical fragment, as the text modulates, yet once more, the first notes of dawn. The long initial sentence reads like *vers libre*, for its rhythms fall into successive cadences which gradually compose the elements of a dawn, whose phenomena are, one after another, emerging in the morning light. Each rhythmic phrase – their unity stressed by internal rhyme or alliteration – constitutes also a sense image, and all but the first are tied, as it were, to the preposition 'de,' whose repetitions form the links which chain the separate sound, sense, and image segments together, both syntactically in the sentence on the page, and also in and to the persona's glance:

> De l'horizon fumé et doré, / la mer peu à peu se démèle; / et des montagnes rougissantes, / des cieux doux et déserts, / de la confusion des feuillages, / des murs, des toits et des vapeurs, / et de ce monde enfin qui se réchauffe / et se résume d'un regard, golfe, campagne, aurore, feux charmants, / mes yeux à regret se retirent et redeviennent les escalves de la table [my slashes].

How close Valéry's prose poetry comes to *vers libre* – how it even becomes that at times and especially at dawn – is illustrated by another morning fragment, also entitled 'Reprise.' Here the poem's rhythm becomes steadily stronger and more regular, so that it developsrapidly from prose into verse, whose lines are made up of the notes we know from the prose aubades:

> *Reprise.*
> Roulements des roues premières. Des revenants laborieux toussent et causent dans la rue probable. Il doit y avoir du soleil frais sur les ordures.
> O vie, ô peinture sur ténèbres!
> Belle matinée, tu es peinte sur la nuit.
> Matin délicieux, qui te peins sur la nuit.
> Ces hirondelles se meuvent comme un son meurt.
> Si haut vole l'oiseau que le regard s'élève à la source des larmes
> (o II, pp 657-8).

While the opening of the poem suggests the temporal nature of its medium and thus the kinship of poetry with music, it also intimates, again, the analogy with painting. For the visual is stressed – 'ce monde ... se résume d'un regard,' 'mes yeux à regret se retirent' – in a text painting the shapes and tones, the textures of dawn. As in the first of the three 'Matin' fragments, Valéry here again approaches a three-dimensional tableau, some of whose components, 'l'horizon fumé et doré,' 'toits et vapeurs,' 'feux charmants,' recall those of the other poem, 'un effet délicieux de lumière,' 'merveille de feu ... de vapeur et d'ardoise,' 'dorure.' But the miracle of the poem is that it reflects both appearance and appearing, the golden surfaces of a world, and their surfacing or emerging from the night.

The poet abandons this young world regretfully, as his eye turns to 'tout un autre monde, un tout autre monde ... le monde des signes sur la table!' From tableau to table – worktable, writing tablet, slab of the tomb – it is upon a two-dimensional plane surface that life, be it that of the mind or of the body, is recorded in signs and symbols, from poem to epitaph, as a lasting trace and vestige of the fleeting. The poem here celebrates its own *écriture*, which transforms the shifting hues and shapes of both the 'inner' and 'outer' moment into the black-on-white signs, the fixed signifiers which preserve and enslave the *signifié*. This celebration is at the same time, however, a lament of a self no longer free; the *ego scriptor* has sold his innocence and purity – Faust-like – to the daemon of Logos, to the compromises, the

falsity, and the powerful magic of language. The saints alone are
pure – Teste neither reads nor writes – and the fallen Angel weeps. In
the prose poem 'London Bridge,' the poet-persona says: 'Voyez-vous
ce monde de flèches et de lettres? ... *In eo vivimus et movemur*' (o II, p
514).[2] The uncommitted beginning, 'commencement sans conditions,'
is one of dawn's mirages, like that of an Eden before the Fall. For, as
Derrida reminds us, *écriture* in its deepest sense is a 'trace' which is
both vestige and origin of a meaningful, a human, world.[3]

As the persona's eyes leave the world outside to become again 'les
escalves de la table,' 'Reprise' signifies the resumption of the daily
labour: 'Que le travail soit avec nous!' Valéry frequently refers to his
daily morning work, the early hours devoted to the *Cahiers*, which he
considered his 'real' task: 'Joie – excitation de surgir à 5 h. et de se
jeter à noter une foule d'idées comme simultanées ... c'est la scin-
tillation de la mer sous le soleil' (c I, p 8). And in a less poetic and more
humorous vain, the sixty-five-year-old poet says: 'Levé avant 5 h. – il
me semble à 8, avoir déjà vécu toute une journée par l'esprit, et
gagné le droit d'être bête jusqu'au soir' (c I, p 10). He even wrote a
prose poem, 'Travail,' which celebrates the ideal and real work of an
artist both possessor and possessed, master and slave, of his art:

> Je t'aime, mon Travail, quand tu es véritablement le mien. Toi, que je
> reconnais sous toutes tes formes. Toi seul, en somme, es vraiment
> moi, que je maîtrise le système vivant des nerfs ou des puissances
> pensantes, que je me sente pénétrant entre mes durées par le plus
> rapide.
>
> Je me possède si tu me possèdes, je suis le maître si je suis ton
> escalve et ton instrument.
>
> Comme le corps du cavalier monté par son idée monte la bête et
> se fait un seul être avec elle,
>
> Comme la barque entre la barre et la toile, contre le vent, par le
> vent.
>
> Oh! ne te laisse pas emporter (comme tant le célèbrent) par la
> seule force qui n'est pas tienne (o I, p 1699).[4]

The written page is an insertion of a world in the universe ('quelle
parenthèse dans l'espace') with its own internal time: 'j'y vois
l'infini des approximations successives.' It is a world conquered and
created – 'cette page toute attaquée d'écriture brouillée de barres et
de surcharges' – out of the contingency of an ever-shifting indeterminate manifold both without and within, the contingency of matter

and of mind, as well as of language itself, by its maker, its author, the *poietes*. In the *Cours de Poétique*, in which Valéry discusses the creative process most fully, he says:

> Le fond de la pensée est toujours désordre, chaos d'images, de mots, d'impulsions, de schèmes qui se forment et se déforment. Mettre sa pensée en un langage, c'est sortir du désordre intérieur pour entrer dans un monde relativement pur, homogène, uniquement composé de mots. Il y a progrès vers la pureté. Ainsi la forme se sépare du fond, comme un produit pur se sépare d'un mélange.[5]

In this creative evolution of cosmos out of chaos – 'l'infini des approximations successives' – the creative spirit is, like God who both creates and sustains the universe, chained to his creation, to that act of making – 'c'est ici que l'esprit à soi-même s'enchaîne' – in which he is both possessor and possessed: 'je me possède si tu me possèdes.'

'L'infini des approximations successives' reaches out beyond the page to all the others, from the poem before us to all the other prose aubades. It describes, in fact, the poetics of a poet for whom perfection is 'le travail qui consiste en une suite interminable de substitutions, toujours en train de se faire, jamais fini, jamais parfait,' a poetics in which 'l'achèvement, indéfiniment ajourné, n'est plus qu'un but délibérément placé dans l'infini.'[6] The prose aubades are themselves successive approximations, 'reprises' arrested only by death; they are what Valéry himself once likened to musical variations on a theme:

> je serais tenté (si je suivais mon sentiment) d'engager les poètes à produire, à la mode des musiciens, une diversité de variantes ou de solutions du même sujet. Rien ne me semblerait plus conforme à l'idée que j'aime à me faire d'un poète et de la poésie (o I, p 1501).

Valéry was always more fascinated by the creative process than by the product, and so in the *Cours de Poétique* he concentrates on poetizing, rather than poetry:

> le mot Poétique n'éveille guère plus que l'idée de prescriptions gênantes et surannées. ... c'est enfin la notion tout simple de FAIRE que je voulais exprimer ... Le Faire, Le *poïein*, dont je veux parler, est celui qui s'achève en quelque oeuvre.[7]

In the 'Poétique' section of the *Cahiers* he likewise insists that 'c'est le faire qui est l'ouvrage, l'objet, à mes yeux capital, puisque la chose faite n'est plus que l'acte de l'autrui,' adding significantly 'cela est du Narcisse tout pur' (c II, p 1022). The poem exists for the reader, who recreates it in the act of reading, but for the poet it remains primarily the reflection of his own creative act. Narcissus is fascinated by his image, that of the *ego scriptor*, which so many pages of the *Cahiers* reflect; in their 'Ego scriptor' section Valéry again explains: 'le travail du poète, le poème m'intéresse moins que les subtilités et les lumières acquises dans ce travail. Et c'est pourquoi il faut *travailler* son poème, – c'est-à-dire se travailler. Le poème sera pour les autres – ... – cependant que le travail sera pour moi' (c I, p 243). It is this 'travail,' both work and torture – *tripaliare* – action and passion, in which the self is indeed both master and slave, which the closing lines of 'Reprise I' celebrate:

> Les dons, les fautes, les repentirs, les rechutes, n'est-ce point sur ce feuillet voué aux flammes tout l'homme moral qui apparaît? Il s'est essayé, il s'est énivré, il s'est déchargé, il s'est fait horreur, il s'est mutilé, il se reprend, il se chérit, et il s'adore.

Here the tension between opposing forces, the good and the bad, remorse and relapse, constitutes the struggle of a purely intellectual ethic in which virtue and excellence are those of the mind – 'presque toute ma morale fut intellectuelle' (c I, p 182). 'Tout l'homme moral' is the *ego scriptor* engaged in his unceasing *'combat avec l'ange'* (c I, p 280), a combat of the self with itself – as is any moral struggle – in which the *moi* conquers and reconstructs itself: 'le travail sacré de l'homme: se reconstruire – c'est la définition de la vie intellectuelle vraie' (c II, p 1386). This internal conflict is stylistically accentuated in our passage by the accumulation of reflexive verbs, whose accelerating rhythm, passing from past perfect to present tense, suggests the secret kinship of this creative *ergon* with the generative energy of Eros. The act of writing in which the writer 'works' both the poem and himself, in which he has passed from self-trial through self-intoxication, self-release, self-loathing, and self-mutilation to the renewal – 'reprise' – of himself, to self-preservation and self-love, is the sublimation of the libidinal to the intellectual which is the origin and end, the source and telos, of art.

From the creative process, in which 'l'esprit à soi-même s'enchaîne,' we proceed in 'Reprise II' to the creative mind itself: 'Esprit.'

Valéry deplored the imprecision of this term, whose meaning he frequently redefined in the *Cahiers*:

> L'esprit est une puissance de prêter à une circonstance actuelle les ressources du passé et les énergies du devenir (c i, p 1322).

Though it is in purely intellectual terms that 'esprit' must be understood in Valéry, its power of generating energy from the past to transmit to the present and thus to 'charge' it for the future, for becoming, makes 'esprit' analogous to the life-creative forces of the universe. The human mind is potentially creative, generative, for it is essentially energy:

> L'esprit est impossible au repos. Tout au plus se compare-t-il parfois à un équilibre stationnaire. C'est un objet étrange qui a pour forme et essence cette impossibilité (c ii, p 624).

In our prose poem, these abstract notions are rendered concrete through the experience of a persona who explores and figuratively expresses the privileged moment – 'un équilibre stationnaire' – when the imminence of the world coincides with that of his mind:

> Esprit. Attente pure, Eternel suspens, menace de tout ce que je désire. Epée qui peut jaillir d'un nuage, combien je ressens l'*imminence*!

As yet another dawn becomes the first, the unique moment out of time – 'Eternel suspens' – in the eternal return and turning of the world, the mind is again pure, universal potentiality, sheer expectation of the 'circonstance actuelle' which will bind it to the temporal, to the world, and to a *moi*. It is (in) suspense, like Damocles under the sword suspended by a hair, its pure universality threatened – imminence-*imminere* – by the particular event that will strike and transform it.

Valéry objectified this moment of expectation elsewhere in both prose and verse; there is a little-known prose poem entitled 'Attente, esquisse d'un poème,' that reads like a sketch to 'Les Pas' (o i, pp 120-1) which, be it about the beloved, inspiration, or both, celebrates above all imminence and 'attente pure':[8]

> Ne hâte pas cet acte tendre,
> Douceur d'être et de n'être pas,

> Car j'ai vécu de vous attendre,
> Et mon cœur n'était que vos pas.

In 'L'Ame et la danse,' Eryximaque exclaims: 'Je n'aime rien tant que ce qui va se produire; et jusque dans l'amour, je ne trouve rien qui l'emporte en volupté sur les tout premiers sentiments. De toutes les heures du jour, l'aube est ma préférée' (o ii, p 159).

The persona of 'Reprise,' 'encore distinct de toute pensée; également éloigné de tous les mots, de toutes les formes qui sont en moi,' is still in that ideal state of mind which we have seen figured by the mathematical 'Zéro'; the perfect neutral circle, both image of and figure for that absence and purity which is at the same time pregnant with undetermined but limitless virtuality.

Not merely the mind, but human sensibility, too, from which the poet also draws and to which he must above all appeal, is rich in unrealized possibilities. In the *Cours de Poétique* lecture devoted to 'le domaine de la sensibilité' Valéry says:

> C'est un fait presque tragique de songer, en regardant un être humain, à ce qu'il peut contenir de possibilités sensorielles: toutes les douleurs, tous les plaisirs et toutes les pensées qui sont possibles en lui. L'instantané n'est rien. L'être humain, dans un instant bien court, n'est rien. *Tout être humain doit être considéré comme une immense virtualité.*

In 'L'Idée fixe,' where Valéry's persona discusses this immense virtuality of both mind and body – 'ma pensée ... dans la pénombre de mon esprit du moment,' 'toute la jouissance, toute la souffrance qu'[on] transporte avec soi, à l'état virtuel' – he develops his own term for it:

> –J'appelle tout ce virtuel dont nous parlions, l'implexe ... j'entends par l'*Implexe*, ce en quoi et par quoi nous sommes éventuels (o ii, pp 232-4).

Valéry frequently defined this key concept in the *Cahiers*:

> L'implexe est ce que nous savons (avec une probabilité énorme) que tirera de nous telle excitation ou atteinte ... Implexe, c'est au fond ce qui est impliqué dans la nature de l'homme ou de moi et qui n'est pas *actuel* (c i, pp 1080-1).

As in our aubade the virtual forms of the outer world are waiting for the rising sun to draw them forth and reveal them in their actuality, so is its morning mind 'expecting,' that is pregnant with a still hidden thought. Like the persona of 'L'Idée fixe,' who bore 'une pensée ... dans la pénombre de [son] esprit,' our matutinal *moi* feels 'une idée inconnue ... encore dans le pli et le souci de [son] front.'

This 'état d'esprit' of potential energy and force, 'l'implexe,' which Valéry celebrated in so many aubades, never ceased fascinating him. It constitutes the climax, moreover, of 'Agathe,' which I touched upon in discussing 'Laure.' In 'Agathe,' which deals with the gradual alterations of the mind during the fragment of a night, the persona arrives, toward the end of her nocturnal voyage, at the same state of 'attente pure': 'je sens sur le front du temps fuir le vague, l'événement venir...' And like our *moi*, who feels a still unknown idea hidden in the furrow of his brow, Agathe, too, knows herself close to a yet unknown idea: 'une perle abstraite roulerait, future dans le repli de la pensée ordinaire' (o II, pp 1390-1). At this point of readiness, both protagonists are in that 'Zéro' state of mind, the 'équilibre stationnaire' of pure absence and neutrality charged with possibility. For Agathe:

> l'ensemble de connaissances diverses, également imminentes qui me constitue ... forme maintenant un système nul ou indifférent à ce qu'il vient produire ou approfondir, quand l'ombre imaginaire doucement cède à toute naissance, et c'est l'esprit (p 1392).

This moment, when the mind is a virtual system, 'un système nul,' independent of its content as well as of any particular existence, is that of the *moi* in 'Reprise,' equidistant still from the world and from itself:

> Je suis encore distinct de toute pensée; également éloigné de tous les mots, de toutes les formes qui sont en moi. Mon œil fixé reflète un objet sans vie; mon oreille n'entend point ce qu'elle entend. O ma présence sans visage, quel regard que ton regard sans choses et sans personne, quelle puissance que cette puissance indéfinissable comme la puissance qui est dans l'air avant l'orage! ... il n'y a point d'homme dans l'homme, et point de *moi* dans le *moi*.'

The 'faceless presence,' the gaze with neither subject nor object, that 'indefinable power,' are those of a god, or of an Angel, 'Esprit pur.'

But in its supreme expectation, the 'Esprit pur,' charged with energy awaiting the spark that will ignite it, is, paradoxically, infinitely more than purely spirit:

> Je suis amour, et soif, et point de nom.

For at the privileged moment which we know, the *moi* is both intellect and affect, pure spirit united to its soul, animus to anima. The golden hour – 'or sur nuit' – is that of Laura's visit: 'Laure ... habite ce silence tout armé d'attentes où je deviens parfois ce que j'attends.'

What is the object of this 'attente,' the event that has neither form nor duration? Its expectation is likened to 'la puissance qui est dans l'air avant l'orage,' and the analogy of the event itself with a stroke of lightning – 'epée qui peut jaillir d'un nuage' – is never stated but implied throughout:

> L'événement qui n'a de figure ni de durée, attaque toute figure et toute durée. Il fait visibles les invisibles et rend invisibles les visibles. Il consume ce qui l'attire, il illumine ce qu'il brise. Me voici, je suis prêt. Frappe.[9]

That which will transform the potential into the kinetic, the igniting spark, the accident which is the substance of the self, is an idea, a thought, the 'master notion.' As the 'idée inconnue' strikes the virtual system of the mind which gives it life, this 'idée maîtresse,' in turn, creates the self in the fulgurant encounter:

> C'est là qu'un événement essentiel quelquefois éclate et me crée.

The shared and reciprocal participation, the copulation, of the idea and the mind in the creative act is stylistically reflected in our passage in the binary structure and equilibrium, in the dynamic balance, of the chiasmatic sentence: '*L'événement qui n'a de figure ni de durée/ attaque toute figure et toute durée. Il fait visibles les invisibles/et rend invisibles les visibles. Il consume ce qui l'attire/il illumine ce qu'il brise.*'

Valéry also celebrated this chance meeting – 'un effet sans cause, un accident qui est ma substance' – of the mind with its master notion in 'Chant de l'idée-maîtresse,' where it is the master notion that sings its ideal union with the mind which gave it birth:

> Je suis la seule idée qui soit conforme à ton être, et toi
> L'homme qui me convient.

> ...
> Je suis venue comme un hasard... ...
> Quel miracle qui me fit être! O circonstance, Humain,
> Seule chance!
>
> ...
> Maintenant, nous nous appartenons. On se confond
> On s'aime (o I, pp 358-9).

From time immemorial poets have celebrated Love – without understanding its mystery.

Both this 'Chant' and our prose poem 'Reprise,' the aubade of and to 'monde' and 'esprit,' are poetic reflections of what Valéry has frequently expressed in the *Cahiers*: 'Il ne faut jamais oublier que nos pensées sont uniquement portées et dévéloppées par les *occasions*. L'accident est ce qu'il y a de plus constant,' and 'toute puissance spirituelle est fondée sur les innombrables hasards de la pensée' (c I, pp 251, 924).

8 'Notes d'aurore'

'Notes d'aurore' (o II, pp 859-60) was first published by the poet as a two-part sequence in 1941 in *Mauvaises Pensées et autres*; it originated from a shorter prose poem, entitled 'Matin,' in a 1916 *Cahier* (c II, pp 1266-7).[1]

The short opening fragment, an exordium to the aubade, acclaims and proclaims the rising sun and the waking voice, the light and language of another dawn and poem. Still another dawn becomes the first, and is the unique, advent-ure and celebration of *hoc die*:

> SALUT ... Choses visibles!
> Je vous écoute, notre *Aujourd'hui* dont l'Exorde est si beau...

L'Exorde,' a classical rhetorical term, introduces the dominant vocabulary cluster of grammar and rhetoric – 'édition,' 'texte,' 'verbe,' 'conjugaison,' 'commenter,' 'proposition,' 'discours' – which is interwoven with the sun-light motif – 'choses visibles,' 'Jour,' 'SOLEIL,' 'couleur,' 'lumière,' 'ombre.' The resulting texture stresses the interdependence of perception and language in experience, as well as that of image and word in the text, the objectification and re-creation of experience in the language of the poem:

> Voici la plus récente édition du vieux texte du Jour: le verbe SOLEIL
> (ce verbe ETRE par excellence) développe les conjugaisons de couleur
> qui lui appartiennent; il commente toutes ces propositions variées de
> lumière et d'ombre dont se fait le discours du temps et du lieu...

The morning's emerging space and time become those of the poem's page, the space and time of the discourse, which is 'le discours du temps et du lieu.' And like each sunrise, every new aubade is 'la plus récente édition du vieux texte du Jour.' The intimate intercourse of world and word creates the meaning and *Bedeutung*, the cosmos and uni-verse of an *aube* and aubade from which the familiar, introspective *moi* appears, paradoxically, absent. In our poem this *moi* becomes extroverted, reflective of external things, 'Choses visibles!' The only 'je' of the entire text – 'je vous écoute, notre Aujourd'hui' – is immediately absorbed by a collective, impersonal 'notre,' and the self becomes 'l'âme,' as universal and objective as '*le* soleil' with which it engages in a matutinal dialogue.

Just as the world's still dormant forms are already latent 'a cette heure,' when the sun begins to illuminate them 'sous l'éclairage presque horizontal,' so is the language that arises to greet and utter them, and which precedes and survives the awakening mind and matter. It both prescribes and describes, guides and traces, the encounter of *corps, esprit,* and *monde,* their hesitations and uncertainty, their ultimate union which marks the beginning of another day of the self and its world, or of the world and its consciousness. For these are at once identical and different, and 'Notes d'aurore' celebrates the latter, the world, more than the former, the self, as self-consciousness is absorbed and its identity submerged in 'world-consciousness.'

The 'Choses visibles!' of the opening is recovered in the second paragraph with '*Voir* se suffit.' To be, 'ETRE,' is light and its perception by the eye of the body and of the mind. Like the eye-hero of 'Purs Drames' – 'la glace mince [qui] imite l'éther absolu, ou lucidement le pense' – so the protagonist of our poem, 'l'âme,' both reflects and thinks the world. And again, the 'fonctionnement' is more significant than the product: 'ce qui est vu vaut moins que le voir même' – as the *poïeïn* is more important to the poet than the poem.

The world calls on the mind through the body's eye and ear, as the poem reflecting these sights and sounds – 'Choses visibles! Je vous écoute,' 'le verbe SOLEIL,' 'le voir,' 'bruit si doux' – is itself both written and spoken, note and song. And the conjunction of the visual and the auditory in a synesthesia of singing gold introduces the Valéryan theme of the music of architecture, celebrated in the poems 'Orphée' and the *mélodrame* 'Amphion':

Des murs quelconques valent un Parthénon, chantent l'or aussi bien.

Every body emerging from the night 'sings the gold,' worships the god – 'or, aurore' – which it reflects, and renders thanks to him for its colour and form, its being:

> Tout corps, miroir du dieu, reporte à lui son existence, rend grâce
> à lui de sa nuance et de sa forme.[2]

As the sun radiates its heat and light, indifferently bestowing energy
and life upon indifferent matter, both that god and his creation are
reflected by a soul and mind which spiritually animate the sunlit
dawn. An impassible world becomes a prayer – 'la première oraison' – because its consciousness, 'l'âme,' as we know from other aubades, wants to worship at this hour: 'je voudrais vous bénir, ô
toutes choses, si je savais...' Light is a metaphor for mind in this poetic
universe because they are analogous in that they are both creative, the
one of the world, the other of the word, its meaning.

We know this dawn's ritual offerings – the flaming tree, the glowing roof tile and gentle morning mists and murmurings – from other
aubades. Our

> là, le pin brûle par la tête; ici la tuile se fait chair. Une charmante
> fumée hésite à s'éloigner du bruit si doux de fuite que fait une eau
> qui coule parmi l'ombre, sous des feuilles,

echoes 'une merveille de feu, de soie, de vapeur et d'ardoise, ensemble
de bruits simples confondus, dorure et murmures,' 'l'horizon fumé et
doré ... des murs, des toits et des vapeurs' of other 'Matins.' The
secretive water hidden by shade and leaves which makes 'so sweet a
noise of flight,' and of which we see a mere mist rising in the sun, is
onomatopoetically reflected by the f-alliterations and vocalic echoes
– 'fumée ... bruit ... fuite ... fait ... feuilles' – as well as stylistically in
the embedded sentence which enfolds and conceals it.

From this still hesitating morning's first appearances, the poet
turns, in the second fragment's long central paragraph, to the equally
hesitant soul and its first emotions:

> L'âme, saisie d'une fraîcheur intime, d'une crainte, d'une tristesse,
> d'une tendresse qui l'opposent encore à tant de puissance croissante,
> se tient un peu à l'écart, dans une réserve inexprimable.

Its innermost, intimate freshness, its fear, its sadness and tenderness,
its chaste reserve on the threshold of the day, are familiar, too, from
other awakenings: 'il s'y mêle de la tristesse, de l'enchantement, de
l'émotion et une sorte de lucidité presque douloureuse,' 'je suis jour
et nuit, j'offre ... une amour infinie, une crainte sans mesure.' Before

surrendering to life, giving itself to feeling the world and letting itself be submerged in its being, the soul wavers, like dawn, between night and day. In the *Cahier* version of our poem, the sadness and tenderness are still attributes of the world, and not of the soul, showing how intimately this morning's *moi* identifies with it:

> Des murs quelconques valent le Parthénon, sont les miroirs voulus, réfléchissent l'être, sont. La fraîcheur, le charme et une crainte, tristesse très pure – baignent (c II, p 1266).

The contrapuntal movement of the poem's two melodies, of the ear and the eye – 'les premières rumeurs dans l'espace qui s'illumine' – now culminates in a harmonious parallel arrangement accentuating the dialectic of being and nothingness:

> les premières rumeurs ... s'établissent sur du silence ... ces formes colorées se posent sur des ténèbres.

Corps, esprit, and *monde* at birth *are* both the night from which they come and the day which they become: 'or et nuit, or sur nuit.'
The 'choses visibles' are as yet unnamed, sheer surfaces of pale pastel shapes and shades, but already in harmony with the soul: the azure is 'pure,' the vermillion 'delicate,' the greens are 'emerald,' and the blues 'hyacinth,' the reds 'chaste.' They are emerging from the dark and as if brushed lightly upon absolute night, just as the soul's languors and reticences are merely tentative still, appearing against the nothingness of sleep. The long sentence with its binary structure and equilibrium reflects that of the moment, the world and its appearance in accord with the soul and its experience of it:

> cet azur si pur, ce vermeil délicat, ces masses d'émeraude et ces pans d'hyacinthe, ces transparences et ces pudeurs carminées sont placées et lavées sur de la nuit absolue;
> ...cette langueur, ces réticences, ces ébauches d'étranges pensées, ces idées singulières ... sont encore des tentatives, des fragments de sa présence, de précaires prémices apparues sur le néant du sommeil...

The precarious beginnings of both the 'aube' and its 'âme' could be swallowed up again by absolute night, 'le soleil' sink into 'le néant du sommeil ... qui pourrait reprendre.' In the 1916 version, the poet had hesitated between 'néant' and 'sommeil' – 'peintes sur le som-meil / néant / encore chaud' – which in our poem have become synonymous.

Again, at dawn in its fragility, the matutinal *moi* in its 'lucidité douloureuse' and 'crainte sans mesure,' so close still to non-being at the moment of birth, knows, 'sent profondément,' that their essence becoming – is the synthesis of absence and presence, containing and comprehending both life and death.

Awakening in and to the young morning's space and time – 'toutes ces propositions variées de lumière et d'ombre dont se fait le dis-cours du temps et du lieu' – the self is no longer in a dream, 'mais les *valeurs* les plus voisines de ces valeurs premières sont valeurs de rêves...' For the distinctive quality of both the noumenal and the phenomenal as they first stir to life in consciousness, their evanescent transience and at the same time vague intimations of immortality, are the stuff that dreams are made of. Birth and the light of the rising sun deceptively hide, 'paint over,' that underside of decay and darkness and death and their monsters which are banned from paradise. All but one! And he is ever-present also in this poetic universe, the Ser-pent of Knowledge, who tempted Faust to the irrespirable heights of the Solitary, and who salutes the 'Great Sun' with his own aubade:

> Grand Soleil, qui sonnes l'éveil
> A l'être, et de feux l'accompagnes,
> Toi qui l'enfermes d'un sommeil
> Trompeusement peint de campagnes,
> Fauteur des fantômes joyeux
> Qui rendent sujette des yeux
> La présence obscure de l'âme,
> Toujours le mensonge m'a plu
> Que tu répands sur l'absolu,
> O roi des ombres fait de flamme! ('Ebauche d'un serpent,' o i, p 139)

Our aubade's conclusion, finally, does not resolve the moment's uncertainty, which in the original *Cahier* version – which still lacks much of the poem's subsequent elaboration – is stressed also non-verbally, by underlining and by double vertical lines in the left mar-gin. This early 'Matin' also more explicitly contrasts the beginning (of the day) with the end (of the night), and sunrise, metaphorically, with sunset: 'le jour ... la veille ... semblent plutôt la fin de quelque chose – le couchant de l'instable.' But both fragments, the early and

the late, spanning over twenty-five years, break off resonating and
reverberating a momentary 'équilibre stationnaire,' dawn's state of
balance between 'le réel' and 'le rien':

> Il n'est pas encore tout à fait sûr que ce jour instant va se confirmer,
> se dégager du possible, s'imposer à ma variété totale ... Le réel
> est encore en équilibre réversible avec le rien de tous ses songes.

9 'Moments'

'Moments,' a sequence of six numbered fragments (o ɪ, pp 311-13) is from *Mélange* (1941), a book which I briefly discussed in connection with the last of the three 'Matin' series of Chapter 5.[1] Each of the six pieces reflects a different moment of the poet's encounter with the world, and the second one, entitled 'Aube,' existed long before publication, in identical form, in a 1920-1 *Cahier* entry (c ɪɪ, p 1272), as did the third, 'Grasse,' in a *Cahier* entry of 1935-6 (c ɪɪ, p 1299). I mentioned 'Moments' in my Introduction, for it is a characteristic example of the Valéryan prose poem sequence, illustrating both the mobile fragment embedded among others of a different period, as well as the truly instantaneous and fragmentary quality of each poem.

The first, third, and fourth moments, each named after the city in which it occurs, recall moreover Valéry's substantial group of prose poems celebrating cities he loved, such as Cannes, Genève, Montpellier; but they remind one above all of the beautiful sequence 'Gênes' from 'Au Hasard et au crayon' of *Rhumbs* (o ɪɪ, pp 598ff.). 'Nice' is another of those poems that, like the fragment 'Reprise' (o ɪɪ, pp 657-8) quoted in Chapter 6, passes from prose into free verse.[2]

In our poem the development of the text marks that of the texture of the night, for all is still dark in the beginning, except for the distant stars: 'Ciel avec peu d'astres, mais l'un splendide dans le pur.' The sky is almost starless, except for that 'splendid' one in 'the pure,' that is the void; but at the same time the word here already suggests that quality peculiar to dawn – 'le mot "Pur" ouvre mes lèvres.' For the night is already preparing for its own extinction, heralded by the refulgence of that bright planet which the persona beholds, 'je ne sais pas qui est celui-ci. ... Planète sans doute.' It might well be Lucifer wandering in the late sky before sunrise, some of whose reflections we have perceived before in the aubades.

The first *vers libre* spells out 'une modification de la nuit qui n'est pas encore l'aube,' and in the second one, the pre-dawn landscape turns into a picture:

> Le tableau est beau, noble.

'Noble' points to the moment's sublimity and, in recalling *noscere*, also suggests an image well known, the familiar 'nudité de la nuit.' The assonance, moreover, of the closed /o's/ – 'aube, tableau, beau' – framed by the two open /o's/ of 'encore' and 'noble' conveys some of its coolness and calm, the repetition of the soft /b's/ the tenderness of the night. The phrase, moreover, contains the anagram of *aube*: 'Le table*au* est *be*au.' The stars are as though mirrored on earth by

> les feux à éclipse, les lignes de la ville marquées par les points
> de feu.

These intermittent lights of the port-town's distant lighthouses wink and twinkle like the far-away stars, while 'à éclipse' further intimates lights gradually declining, both those marking the city's lines, and those in the morning sky.

In the following line the persona becomes as universal as the setting and the moment, the point in time which he reflects: 'Man' at the intersection between night and day, between earth and sky:

> L'homme *pèse* ce qu'il *voit* et en est *pesé*.

Here the poet explicitly paints the image of the balance with its two suspended scales, figuring that dynamic state of equilibrium of opposing forces which characterizes these aubades. We saw the preceding sequence, 'Notes d'aurore,' conclude on the momentary 'équilibre stationnaire' between 'le réel' and 'le néant.' The *moi* of the 'A B C' trilogy was – like the hour surrounding him – composed of an inner tension of opposites, 'je dors et je veille, je suis jour et nuit ... amour infinie, crainte sans mesure ... femme endormie, ange fait de lumière,' – a 'gray-haired child' and a moment of lucidity and mystery. But expressions of this balance and tension are almost ubiquitous in the prose poems. In the second of the 'Trois Réveils,' we beheld the persona's mind as a stage on which opposing forces were momentarily interlocked in a precarious equilibrium, reflected stylistically in the symmetrically balanced structure of the sentence: 'il y a conflit parfois entre *ce qui pense* et qui *veut* ne plus penser, mais dormir, et *ce qui est pensé* et qui *veut* se développer – voir son avenir.' The symmetrically balanced sentence, with its syntactically parallel constructions, peculiar to the dawn prose poems, was again elaborated – with a temporal dimension – in one of the 'Matins': 'ici, unies au jour qui jamais ne fut encore, les parfaites pensées qui jamais ne seront.' The second of those two sequences, finally, most forcefully stressed the balance of night and day, the dialectic of darkness and light, in a statement which itself constitutes an equation, thus underlining the binary structure of both the perceiving mind and its language: 'il y a un instant où l'on dirait que la nuit se fait voir à la lumière, comme l'esprit au réveil fait voir la naissance, l'inexistence et les rêves à la première lucidité.' And in the second fragment of these 'Moments,' a moment both 'final' and 'initial,' this dialectic will be taken up again.

Our first 'Moment,' however, *images* this persistent motif, which gradually grows into a central theme of the aubades, in the balance, at once image and concept. Man, in his first encounter with the world and himself, both weighs and is weighed by what he perceives:

> Quand il ne peut égaler ni fuir ce qui est dans l'autre *plateau*, c'est beau.

'Plateau' is underlined, as were 'pèse, voit' and 'pesé' in the preceding line, to emphasize the image and notion of the scale balancing its two trays, whose momentary equilibrium is now depicted in 'ne fuir ... ni égaler,' as above in 'pèse ... pesé.' A secondary meaning of 'plateau,' moreover, is 'a momentary phase of stability'; and how rich this is in virtual tension we know from other aubades. For at this privileged moment, when the self also contains the world – 'Tout l'univers chancelle et tremble sur ma tige' – by which it is contained, then 'le Tout est un germe – le Tout ressenti sans parties.'

As dawn merely suggests in their virtuality those forms which the oncoming day will then reduce to their concrete and mortal limitations, so the awakening *moi*, at this first moment, forgets his own mortality. When the world thus appears most 'beautiful,' the self seems most powerful, and the poet dreams about the ideal poem:

> Je pense au poème de l'Intellect.

The references to this 'poème de l'Intellect' are numerous and widely scattered throughout the *œuvre* as well as the *Cahiers*, where it is at times conceived dramatically, at others lyrically, or again in an expository vein. A 1919 entry reads: 'j'ai vu une pièce terrible – toute angoisses, hontes, intensités et je me dis: Faire aussi *fort* que tout cela, aussi poignant et empoignant, mais dans l'ordre de l'intelligence' (c I, p 241). Many years later, the poet notes: 'ce que j'ai envisagé l'un des premiers, peut-être, c'est la "sensibilité de l'intellect" – ce qu'il y a d'amour, de jalousie, de piété, de désir, de jouissance, de courage, d'amertume, et même d'avarice, de luxure ... dans les choses de l'intelligence' (c I, p 623). How he would draw from these very *Cahiers* to create this work celebrating the mind – as we have seen him do repeatedly with the aubades – is evident from another note, in which he envisions a treatise on the intellectual life: 'traité de la vie intellectuelle – Mystique intellectuelle à former de bien des remarques prises dans ces cahiers – Les malheurs de l'esprit. Ses joies. Sa place – Sa nullité – Ses exigences – Ses défenses' (c II, p 1321). 'L'Homme et la coquille' opens with 's'il y eût une poésie des merveilles et des émotions de l'intellect (à quoi j'ai songé toute ma vie)...' (o I, p 886), and in the 'Note et digression,' Valéry tells us that he sees in his imaginary Léonard – the projection of an ideal self – the protagonist of the ideal poem: 'je vois en lui le personnage principal de cette Comédie intellectuelle qui n'a pas jusqu'ici rencontré son poète, et qui serait pour mon goût bien plus précieuse encore que *La Comédie humaine*, et même que *La Divine Comédie*' (o I, p 1201).

Finally, Maurice Toesca relates a conversation he had with the poet in 1944, in which Valéry mentioned to him that *La Soirée avec Monsieur Teste* was to become part of the great work, that 'roman d'un cerveau,' some of the numerous allusions to which I have just recalled.[3] Valéry's prose poem 'Agathe,' to which I have referred several times in discussing these aubades, was to become one of this *œuvre*'s chapters or fragments. I mentioned in 'Fragments' that Valéry had created Teste, a monster of pure Intellect, to exorcise another part of himself, those emotions and the anguish which threatened him, sometimes even at dawn – 'Angoisse, mon véritable métier.' Teste, a character created 'par le fractionnement d'un être réel dont on extrairait les moments les plus intellectuels pour en composer le tout de la vie d'un personnage imaginaire,' confesses to idealizing his mind, his intellect: 'je confesse que j'ai fait une idole de mon esprit, mais je n'en ai pas trouvé d'autre.' It is no surprise, then, that the poet, having created that curious 'personnage' and his 'Cycle Teste,' some of whose fragments go back as far as 1896 (*La Soirée*) while others were written some thirty years later, should also muse about 'poetizing' this tendency of himself. And this he does, of course,

all along. Both the temptations and the threats of 'l'Esprit pur' per-
vade his major poems, 'La Jeune Parque,' and the *Charmes* from
'Aurore' to 'Le Cimetière marin.'[4]

But nowhere is the theme of the Intellect as fully and persistently
elaborated as in the prose aubades, for their central theme is 'la
sensibilité de l'intellect.' These morning prose poems celebrate both
'l'intellect' and its feelings, the 'Esprit pur' in its attempts to transcend
the world on which it depends, and 'ce qu'il y a d'amour, de jalousie,
de piété, de désir, de jouissance, de courage, d'amertume...' The
prose aubades are not Teste's, but Valéry's 'poèmes de l'intellect.'

The second fragment of the sequence is again an aubade, and it
observes a 'moment' which both is and is not, for it is be-coming. Just
as the preceding piece opened upon a 'not-yet dawn' with 'une modification de la nuit qui n'est pas encore l'aube,' so this beginning dwells
on the waning of the moon, which already is, and at the same time,
paradoxically, is not yet the privileged moment we know:

> Aube – Ce n'est pas l'aube. Mais le déclin de la lune...

In this beginning – of a poem and of a day – the poet becomes his own
antagonist, as he must objectify what he experiences in a language
which cannot express that experience. This theme links our fragment
to another Valéryan prose sequence, 'Magie,' in whose opening passages the poet appears caught in similar contradictions, those imposed
by his very medium:

> A ce moment, le coq chanta et ne chanta pas, et ce n'était pas un
> coq – et peut-être pas un moment. Le vent fraîchit et ne fraîchit
> pas – et le ciel tout blanc d'astres n'avait pas existé. On l'avait
> récusé à temps, et ainsi de toutes choses.
> Et à chaque instant, ce qui fut n'avait pas été (o ii, p 858).

It is not surprising that both our 'Aube,' which is not an *aube*, as well
as the opening moment of 'Magie,' which perhaps was not a moment,
should bring to mind Rimbaud's *Illuminations*, – for example 'Veil-
lées' – in which that poet attempts to remake the language to con-
form to *his* vision.[5] Valéry frequently discusses the tension between
vision and expression in the *Cahiers*: 'Le langage me subit et me fait
subir. Tantôt je le plie à ma vue, tantôt il transforme ma vue' (c i,
p 393).

The dying moon of 'Moments,' announcing the day about to be
born,

> la lune, perle rongée, glace fondante, et une lueur *mourante* à qui le
> jour *naissant* se substitue peu à peu – [my italics]

is the same as that of the last piece of the 'A B C' trilogy: 'la lune ce
fragment de glace fondante ... cet objet céleste de substance étince-
lante et mourante, tendre et froide qui va se dissoudre insensible-
ment.' For that fragment, like ours, elaborates the 'jeu de contrastes,'
the antitheses which are the essence of the 'moment':

> J'aime ce moment si pur, *final, initial*. Mélange de calme, de
> renoncement, de négation [my italics].

This 'renoncement' and 'abandon,' the resignation and yielding, are
those of both the night and the consciousness which animates and
personifies it. It is a 'drowsy setting' of the nocturnal and the soul, as
the latter paradoxically awakens to 'tuck in' night and sleep to rest,
and dreams yield to the 'real dream' of a new day:

> Abandon – On referme respectueusement la nuit. On la replie, on la
> borde. C'est le coucher et l'assoupissement du moi le plus seul. Le
> sommeil va se reposer. Les songes le cèdent au rêve réel.

The hermetic *moi* of the night is being put behind now.

As the body stirs to life, the assonating and alliterating double sub-
jects of the two sentences which describe it stress that body's bilateral
structure:

> L'agitation et l'animation vont naître. Les muscles, les machines
> vont envahir le pays de l'être. Le réel semble hésiter encore.

Stylistically, the passage recalls a similar one from one of the 'Matin'
fragments rendering the same phenomenon: 'le corps s'étire, se
tourne et se retourne, cherche une torsion et une tension qui lui fassent reconnaître sa place dans lui-même.'

Finally the sun rises, like an oriflamme unfurling at the whistle-
blast:

> Le Zaïmph se déroule, et, au coup de sifflet, va être hissé aux
> vergues, aux arbres, aux toits, occuper le ciel.

The Carthaginian word 'Zaïmph' – 'voile sacré de la Tanit de
Carthage' (Larousse) – reminds us that Valéry's is a Mediterranean

sun, which is further intimated by 'hissé aux vergues,' the mainyards of ships recalling the sea. 'Zaïmph' further suggests the sun's role as giver of life – 'on est fécondé, gros d'un jour nouveau' – for the cult of the Tanit of Carthage celebrated Astarte, the Phoenician goddess of fertility and sexual love.[6]

Our third 'Moment' is not dawn, but a fragment of a morning, at Grasse, not far from Nice. It is, moreover, a pure picture and therefore entirely lacking in verbs. The poet himself tells us its manner:

> Grasse – Neige peu dense sur le sol – pas sur les arbres – effet à la Breughel. Le sol frotté et non couvert.
> Ce matin, soleil.
> Impression frileuse et dorée – sensation d'enfance en moi.
> Mélange d'excitation et de mélancolie.

The rare and thin snow in the morning sun of the southern city recalls childhood surprises and the excitement at snow fallen gently during the night.[7] The cold and golden impression, 'impression frileuse et dorée,' echoing 'le sol frotté,' intimates with the repetition of the /f's/, /r's/ and /s's/ the somewhat granular texture of the scene, both the 'real' one – of the poem – and that of a Breughel painting. And as the child returns in the man, there mounts that melancholy which we know from other aubades: 'Ma jeunesse jadis a langui et senti la montée des larmes, vers la même heure, et sous le même enchantement ... je me vois à côté de ma jeunesse...'

The fourth 'moment,' a little later in the day and again at Grasse, reintroduces the morning bird, a motif discussed earlier, when I noted the fascination that birds held for Valéry because of their freedom of movement and their song: 'chant et mobilité.'[8] In 'Reprise' we saw the morning soul soaring on swallows' wings:

> Ces hirondelles se meuvent comme un son meurt.
> Si haut vole l'oiseau que le regard s'élève à la source des larmes.

This fragment also celebrates the swallow, and the melodious '*belle* hi*rondelle* bleue et or' [my italics] renders the sweeping curves of its flight with the sound look of its signifiers:

> Grasse. – Six heures et quart – Tout à coup une belle hirondelle bleue et or brusquement se jette dans ma chambre, fait trois tours, retrouve la petite fenêtre carrée et fuit, comme crevant l'image du pays, par ce trou de lumière où elle s'était précipitée en tant que trou

d'ombre, et qu'il lui a suffi de virer de bord pour la changer en
lumière, en autre monde...
    Peut-être ne l'a-t-elle pas reconnu?

In our sequence, the episode of the swallow diving into, circling,
and soaring out of the poet's room serves once again to play on the
dialectical tension between night and day, darkness and light. In balancing 'trou de lumière' with 'trou d'ombre,' even changing the one
into the other, and at the same time placing in equilibrium the 'inside'-'outside' dichotomy, the text stresses the dependence of one side
upon the other, and again the image of the balance comes before the
mind's eye, with 'esprit' and 'monde' suspended, as are night and day
at dawn. The 'inside' is meaningless without, thus depends on, the
'outside,' and the mind is as much in the world as the world is in the
mind.

I have commented several times on the fragmentary and instantaneous quality of many of Valéry's prose poems. This characteristic is
notably evident in the fifth of the 'Moments':

> Il y a des arbres, des fleurs, un chien, des chèvres, le soleil, le paysan
> et moi, et la mer au loin; et nous tous ensemble convenons que le
> passé n'existe plus.

This is a 'pur regard,' though an artistic one, at a world of which the
beholding eye is a part, in a pure present, excluding both past and
future, an instant now. At the same time this 'Moment' prepares the
next, for it establishes the 'pastoral' mood, a Theocritus's charming
illusion of the innocence of youth and of nature, appropriate to the
beginning of a day.

The kinship of fragments v and vi is borne out, moreover, by the fact
that they were originally one, in inverted order, so that our v was the
concluding paragraph of vi, the two together forming one piece in a
1923 *Cahier* (c i, pp 96-7). Thus we have here again a perfect example
of the mobility of the poetic prose fragment within the *œuvre*.

In the sixth 'Moment' of the sequence, the persona is, as he was in
the first, a poet-persona, who speaks about 'singing' and painting
what he sees:

> Je vois la nature â ma façon. Je pense à ceci en regardant une
> grande chèvre dans les oliviers. Elle mordille, bondit. *Virgile*, pen-
> sai-je. Jamais l'idée de peindre ou chanter cette chèvre ne me fût
> venue.

> Virgile prouve que l'on peut en faire quelque chose.
>
> Je la regarde donc. Elle cesse aussitôt d'être chèvre – et l'olivier cesse d'être olivier. Ici commence *moi* – c'est-à-dire un regard que je voudrais bien définir.

The text's only two italicized words, '*Virgile*' and '*moi*' underline the association of the poet-persona with the renowned predecessor, to whom Valéry refers frequently throughout the *oeuvre*, and one of whose works he had translated. I am referring to the poet's 'vers blanc' translation of Vergil's *Bucolics*, which occupied him from 1942 to 1944, and which was published posthumously in 1955 with Valéry's preface (o I, pp 207-81). In that preface, 'Variations sur les *Bucoliques*,' he stresses, as he does in our prose poem, the divergence of taste between the Mantuan and himself: 'je confesse que les thèmes bucoliques n'excitent pas furieusement mon courage. ... je suis né dans un port' (o I, pp 208-9). And in the prose poem 'Nage,' which of course celebrates water, the poet again says: 'je ne connais rien aux moissons, aux vendanges. Rien pour moi dans les *Géorgiques*' (o II, p 667).

What Valéry and Vergil do have in common, however, is their *métier*: they are poets. And what fascinates Valéry, as pointed out in detail in Chapter 6, is not so much the poem as its making, 'la notion tout simple de FAIRE ... Le Faire, le *poïeïn* ... qui s'achéve en quelque oeuvre.' As the poet-persona beholds the goat among the olive trees, the pastoral Vergil comes to his mind, and the challenge: 'Virgile prouve que l'on peut en *faire* quelque chose' [my italics]. The poetic 'regard' – 'je vois,' 'en regardant,' 'je la regarde,' 'ici commence *moi* – c'est-à-dire un regard' – is pure as 'l'oeil pur' of 'Purs Drames,' but it is, as we have said, *artistic*. It transforms nature, and its definition is the poem.

As our first 'Moment' closed with the persona musing about a poem to be written – 'je pense au poème de l'Intellect' – so the final one ends similarly, with the poet-persona dreaming about a poem, 'un regard que je voudrais bien définir.'

10 Petits Poèmes abstraits

In January 1932, Valéry published in *La Revue de France* a sequence of four numbered prose poems, entitled 'Avant toute Chose,' 'L'Unique,' 'Accueil du jour' and 'La Rentrée.'[1]The first of these, again a mobile fragment, later reappeared as Part I of the sequence 'Méditation avant pensée.'[2]

'Avant toute Chose' again observes the privileged first moment of the self and the day, its anteriority and priority to anything that might come after. The 'aurores' of this poetic universe, I have said repeatedly, are the golden and mythic Eden 'au commencement,' at the beginning of a world whose words and figures, whose realization and reality are but a falling off from that former state. Before all things – and thoughts – pure hope and desire and the love of loving fill the mind and soul, and form the question which precedes the quest:

> Est-il espoir plus pur, plus délié du monde, affranchi de moi-même – et toutefois possession plus entière – que je n'en trouve avant le jour, dans un moment premier de proposition et d'unité de mes forces, quand le seul désir de l'esprit, qui en précède toutes les pensées particulières, semble préférer de les suspendre et d'être amour de ce qui aime?

At this 'moment premier ... d'unité de mes forces,' mind and soul are one, so that 'l'esprit' and 'l'âme' are synonymous:

> L'âme jouit de sa lumière sans objets. Son silence est le total de sa parole, et la somme de ses pouvoirs compose ce repos. Elle se sent également éloignée de tous les noms et de toutes les formes. Nulle figure encore ne l'altère ni ne la contraint. Le moindre jugement entachera sa perfection.

The 'esprit pur,' still free of 'toutes les pensées particulières,' *is* 'l'âme' rejoicing in its 'lumière sans objets.' And in this state of mind and soul, the *moi*, 'loosened from the world' and 'freed from the self,' equidistant 'de tous les noms' (the word) and 'de toutes les formes' (the world), recalls the matutinal *moi* of 'Reprise ɪɪ': 'je suis encore distinct de toute pensée; également éloigné de tous les mots, de toutes les formes qui sont en moi.' This is again the ideal 'Zéro' state and moment, 'qui ... exprime le sans-attribut, ni image, ni valeur du Moi pur.'

The moment 'avant toute chose' is pre-Edenic, when the world is still immanent in the Divine, a beginning *before* the Word. The Creator, we recall, 'se fit Celui qui dissipe/En conséquences son Principe,/En étoiles, son Unité.' In a 1920 *Cahier* entry, Valéry muses, 's'il y avait un Dieu, il n'y aurait que lui, et pas de monde' (c ɪɪ, p 602). The *moi* 'avant le jour' aspires after that universality which refuses any particular proposition, be it of perception or thought, and knows nothing but the potential, 'puissance':

> Par la vertu de mon corps reposé, j'ignore ce qui n'est point *puissance*, et mon attente est un délice qui se suffit; elle suppose, mais elle diffère, tout ce qui peut se concevoir.

As in 'Reprise ɪɪ' the mind suspended all specific thoughts, and the soul all objects, so here the *moi* defers all that can be perceived.

Valéry fully developed this notion, which grows into a major theme of the aubades, in 'Note et digression,' whose occasion and pretext is the intellectual hero Léonard, 'un *modèle* psychologique' and ideal projection of the self. In that text, we find the same ideal reduction as in 'Avant toute Chose': '*l'homme de l'esprit* doit se réduire sciemment à un refus indéfini d'être quoi que ce soit' (o ɪ, p 1225), and this anti-existentialist, anti-phenomenological progression – 'la conscience est toujours conscience de quelque chose' – a progressive depersonalization, aspires after an ideal universal self:

> L'oeuvre capitale et cachée du plus grand esprit n'est-elle pas de soustraire cette attention substantielle à la lutte des vérités ordinaires? Ne faut-il pas qu'il arrive à se définir, contre toutes choses ... ce qui lui confère une généralité presque inconcevable, et le porte en quelque manière, à la puissance de l'univers correspondant (o ɪ, p 1228)?

Our poem's persona rejoices:

> Quelle merveille qu'un instant universel s'édifie au moyen d'un
> homme, et que la vie d'une personne exhale ce peu d'éternel!

In this state of mystic detachment and ecstasy, which brings to
mind a similar moment of the 'A B C' trilogy, Man invents the most
mysterious and the most daring words of his language:[3]

> N'est-ce point dans un état si détaché que les hommes ont inventé
> les mots les plus mystérieux et les plus téméraires de leur langage?

And they must be those of prayer. 'Elevez ce qui est mystère en vous
à ce qui est mystère en soi,' the poet had said in the 'c' fragment.

Prayer was the only phenomenon of religion in a formal sense ac-
cessible to the agnostic Valéry: 'la prière est peut-être ce qu'il y a
uniquement de *réel* dans une religion' (c II, p 605).[4] His reflections
about religion are numerous throughout the *Cahiers*, spanning his
entire mature life (the *Thêta* entries from 1896 to 1945, c II, pp
565-718), and since they consist of unresolved questions and meditations rather than answers, it would be audacious to pronounce oneself
on Valéry's religious beliefs or attitudes. At one point, however, he
expresses a 'loss' of God: 'j'ai perdu mon Dieu il y a longtemps – au
moment où je me suis aperçu qu'il était en moi, ce moi que j'ai
toujours méprisé' (c II, p 569); at another, he voices a certain nostalgia for this lost God: 's'il y avait un Dieu, je ne vivrais que pour
lui – quelle curiosité, quelle passion m'inspirerait un si grand
être, – quelle science autre que la sienne? Mais s'il y en avait un, je le
percevrais, je le sentirais en quelque manière, et je ne sens rien' (c II, p
601). He most consistently appears to believe that the Divine can
never be *known*, only *felt*, that it exists, like evil, within: 'La plus
grossière des hypothèses est de croire que Dieu existe objectivement
... Oui! il existe et le Diable, mais en nous! ... En deux mots: Dieu est
notre *idéal particulier*. Satan ce qui tend à nous en détourner' (o II, p
1431).

It is perhaps for this reason, then, that this 'mystère' within is felt
most intensely at dawn, when the self attains the summit of being. For
what is it that Man calls Divine, if not this 'indefinable' power, which
the poet recalls again and again in the aubades?:

> O moment, diamant du Temps! ... Je ne suis que détail et soins
> misérables hors de toi.
>   Sur le plus haut de l'être, je respire une puissance indéfinissable
> comme la puissance qui est dans l'air avant l'orage.

Again 'Reprise II' comes to mind, because exactly the same words, the same phrase, appeared embedded in, and as a fragment of, a paragraph of that poem:

> Je suis encore distinct de toute pensée; également éloigné de tous les mots, de toutes les formes qui sont en moi. ... O ma présence sans visage, quel regard que ton regard sans choses et sans personne, quelle puissance que *cette puissance indéfinissable comme la puissance qui est dans l'air avant l'orage*! ... il n'y a point d'homme dans l'homme ... [my italics].

Just as in prayers certain words and phrases become formulaic, so in these aubades, which become something like a ritual celebration of the poet's 'veilles matinales.' Valéry, who said, 'j'étais fait pour chanter Matines,' himself suggests that his morning poems are analogous to 'Matins,' the daily observance of the first canonical hour. There is in the *Cahiers* a little aubade, entitled 'Intellectual Morning Prayer,' which reflects the ideas and sentiments, the tonality, of 'Avant toute Chose':

> Prière intellectuelle du matin –
> Avant le commencement –
> Avant la Création –
> La Puissance d'abord se découvre –
> Quelques éclairs dispersés, divers – percent la nue et le sommeil
> Comme pour établir le monde et l'espace où l'on va se mouvoir et
> choisir un chemin –
> Froideur et simplicité de cette aurore – oraison (c II, pp 1271-2).

And a 'Psaume' of those years is, appropriately, about God:

> Psaume
> Tu n'adoreras pas les dieux des autres;
> ...
> Tu connaîtras le Tien à sa simplicité,
> Il ne te proposera pas des énigmes vides
> ...
> Il sort de toi comme tu sors de ton sommeil
> ...
> Cache ton dieu. Que ce dieu soit ton trésor – que ton trésor soit ton
> dieu (c II, p 1284).

Valéry's God is hidden in the aubades, as he is in the *moi* which sings them.

The first fragment closes with the *moi* at its highest point, 'sur le plus haut de l'être,' feeling the promise of the world and itself, the privileged moment which in one of the 'Matins' was objectified in the metaphor of the seed: 'en germe, éternellement germe, le plus haut degré universel d'existence.'

The world – like the self – is pure possibility: 'before all things' and their existence, soul and eye rejoice in light without objects, seeing rather than the seen:

> Je ressens l'imminence ... Je ne sais ce qui se prépare; mais je sais
> bien ce qui se fait: *Rendre purement possible ce qui existe; réduire ce qui se*
> *voit au purement visible* – telle est l'oeuvre profonde.

This 'oeuvre profonde' echoes 'l'oeuvre capitale' from 'Note et digression,' quoted above: 'l'oeuvre capitale et cachée du plus grand esprit n'est-elle pas de soustraire cette attention à la lutte des vérités ordinaires? ... à se définir contre toutes choses?' It also recalls the early 'Purs Drames,' and the artist's exhortation to reduce the images (objects) of his vision, 'corrompues encore par la certitude de leurs éléments,' to simpler, purer origins: 'il n'y a que les lignes simples.' In that first of Valéry's aubades, we saw the reminiscence of Eden ideally reduced to a pure, harmonious line, 'une ligne sur l'espace de couleur céleste ou vitale.'

In the next fragment of our sequence, 'L'Unique,' the One without equal is again the first day rising paradoxically for a thousandth time:

> Mille fois, j'ai déjà ressenti l'Unique...
> Mille fois, plus de mille fois, ce dont l'essence est d'être unique...

The bipolarity of 'mille fois' and 'unique,' stressed by repetition, is then further elaborated by the shift from monologue to dialogue, the *moi*'s 'je' to its 'tu,' and that of cognizance from the self to the world, the 'unique' dawn:

> 'Tu le laisses toujours ne pas te reconnaître!...

The sixty-year-old poet's persona is again the 'enfant aux cheveux gris' of the 'c' poem, for whom the morning rises both new and long known, so that the light-darkness dichotomy which makes up the

tension of the moment – 'ce moment si pur, *final, initial'* – parallels
that of the self in a reciprocal reflection of 'inner' and 'outer,' the soul
reflecting the world which mirrors it.

Our text recalls the young Fate's weariness after too many days of
her life,

> Car l'œil spirituel sur les plages de soie
> Avait déjà vu luire et pâlir trop de jours
> Dont je m'étais prédit les couleurs et les cours,

who is then, however, reborn to salute the new, divine dawn:

> Salut! Divinités par la rose et le sel,
> Et *les premiers jouets de la jeune lumière*,
> Iles (o I, pp 101, 106) [my italics]!

It also brings to mind the old Faust, whom we followed in our discussion of another aubade ('Trois Réveils') to the arid nihilism of the
Solitaire's mountain top. Faust's wisdom is to live each one of the
uncountable breaths of his life uniquely, as for the first time:

> JE RESPIRE ... J'ouvre profondément *chaque fois, toujours pour la première
> fois*, ces ailes intérieures qui battent le temps vrai (o II, p 322) [my
> italics].

In 'L'Homme et la coquille,' where Valéry speaks about the *Urfor-
men* of art and of artistic vision, he exhorts us to awaken the child in
us for a renewed vision of the world:

> Nous refusons à chaque instant d'écouter l'ingénu que nous por-
> tons en nous. Nous réprimons *l'enfant qui nous demeure et qui veut
> toujours voir pour la première fois* (o I, pp 890-1) [my italics].

This renewed vision is the theme also of the 'Introduction a la
Méthode de Léonard de Vinci,' Valéry's ideal 'phenomenology of
perception,' in which he says:

> Certains hommes ressentent, avec une délicatesse spéciale, la
> volupté de l'*individualité* des objets. Ils préfèrent avec délices,
> dans une chose, *cette qualité d'être unique – qu'elles ont toutes* (o I,
> p 1170) [last italics mine].

Here he stresses the same paradox as that of our poem, that uniqueness which all things have, like the uniqueness of each one of all the
uncountable dawns. The miracle of the 'first time for the thousandth
time' which is the essence of love and of the privileged golden moment of 'aurore,' is also that of artistic contemplation, that of the poem
rising again and again, and each time uniquely, from its ashes: 'le
poème ne meurt pas pour avoir servi; il est fait expressément pour
renaître de ses cendres et redevenir indéfiniment ce qu'il vient
d'être' (o I, p 1373). It is the moment created by the 'ardent' Athikté
in her dance, which Phèdre ('L'Ame et la danse') likens to a rising
flame: 'On croirait que la danse lui sort du corps comme une flamme!'
Socrates then develops the simile into a metaphor for the privileged
moment, the flame:

> O Flamme, toutefois! ... Chose vive et divine!...
>   Mais qu'est-ce qu'une flamme, ô mes amis, si ce n'est *le moment*
> même? – Ce qu'il y a de fol, et de joyeux, et de formidable dans
> l'instant même! ... Flamme est l'acte de ce moment qui est entre la
> terre et le ciel. O mes amis, tout ce qui passe de l'état lourd à l'état
> subtil, passe par le moment de feu et de lumière...(o II, p 171).

Thus, in a suggestion of alchemical imagery, the soul upon awakening
passes from 'l'état lourd' (of night and sleep) 'à l'état subtil' as it
rises to 'le moment de feu et de lumière.' In our poem, the poet apostrophizes the moment:

> O moment, diamant du Temps!...

Valéry's aubades, disseminated and hidden throughout his poetic
universe, are the diamonds: precious, crystalline fragments, conden-
sations of time, *moments privilégiés.*

   It is the mind's capacity to forget, to obliterate, that enables it to
recreate, and in this it imitates nature – the 'aurores' – in its eternal
cycle of death and resurrection:[5]

> Il y a donc, dans la substance d'un homme, une vertu d'effacement,
> sans laquelle un seul jour suffirait, épuiserait, consumerait l'attrait
> du monde; une seule pensée annulerait l'esprit?

In the following paragraph, the poet suggests the image of the legendary phoenix rising in renewed freshness from its own ashes, which
he elsewhere applies to poetry, in evoking the matutinal soul's thirst
and joy as it arises from the night of its forgetfulness and extinction:[6]

> Mais une soif de connaître, une joie de se sentir venir quelque pro-
> chaine Idée – de sentir s'éclairer peu à peu un royaume d'intelli-
> gence – renaît indéfiniment des cendres secrètes de l'âme.
> Chaque aurore est première. L'idée qui vient crée un homme
> nouveau.

In this awakening, 'connaître' and 'sentir' become one, as spirit and
soul, animus and anima, embrace. 'L'âme,' like a joyous bride, *feels*
and 'thirsts for' the approaching Master Notion, 'quelque prochaine
Idée – ... l'idée qui vient.' The consummation of their union will
create 'un homme nouveau.'

Valéry never tired of celebrating this moment of anticipation –
'frisson préalable à la mer' – of the creative copulation of the soul,
the 'esprit' and its Idea. We saw the theme most fully elaborated in
'Reprise II,' where the expectation – 'attente pure' – was also a loving
and a thirsting: 'je suis amour, et soif, et point de nom,' and the self a
readiness: 'me voici, je suis prêt. Frappe.' Our poem's 'l'idée qui
vient crée un homme nouveau' echoes the 'un événement essentiel
quelquefois éclate et me crée' of the other fragment. Again
'Agathe's' quest for the 'perle abstraite' comes to mind, and the 'Chant
de l'idée maîtresse,' the epithalamion which sings the union of
mind and idea: 'Maintenant nous nous appartenons. On se confond/
On s'aime.' Traditionally, aubades were love poems: so are Valéry's.

In the following section, the motif of cyclical return – or 'how can
one always fall in, rise to, love again?' – is taken up once more, this
time couched in the mystical language announced in the preceding
fragment. 'Les mots les plus mystérieux et les plus téméraires' are:
'those mysterious altars,' 'our offered life,' 'the idols,' 'spiritual acts,'
and 'extraordinary prayers,' and hyperbolic capitalization marks the
divinities adored: 'pure Promise,' 'infinite degrees of Knowledge,' and
'the Intellect.'

> Mais comment se peut-il que je m'ignore et m'abolisse à ce point que
> l'espoir redevienne, et redore toujours les hauts frontons de la pure
> Promesse, les degrés infinis de la Connaissance, et ces autels
> mystérieux où notre vie offerte se change en fumée au pied des
> idoles de l'Intellect, où des actes spirituels et des prières extraordi-
> naires transforment notre amour, notre sang, notre temps, en œuvres
> et en pensées?

The text suggests a mystic's death – 'je m'abolisse' – and resurrection,
a dying in order to be reborn, a voluntary death for the sake of gaining

a new existence. It is a literary theme and a spiritual experience as old
as mythology; its ritual observance by the matutinal *moi* celebrates
the Poet's participation in that Orphic descent and return.[7] For that
legend tells of a sacrifice, like ours in which 'our offered lives' are
turned into 'votive smoke,' and 'our love – Eurydice – lifeblood and
duration' transformed into art: 'en oeuvres et en pensées.'

With its 'lofty pediments,' 'endless staircases,' and 'mysterious
altars,' our text also suggests the architectural Orpheus, a major
Valéryan theme already touched upon in 'Notes d'aurore.' The
theme was first elaborated in the early poetic prose essay 'Paradoxe
sur l'architecte' of 1891 and the sonnet 'Orphée' of the same year,
later in the Socratic dialogue 'Eupalinos ou l'architecte' of 1921, and
finally the 'mélodrame' 'Amphion' of 1931. For architecture was to
Valéry the realization of creative thought in *œuvre* par excellence.

This richly allusive passage, moreover, with 'ces autels mystérieux
où notre vie offerte se change en fumée' recalls another builder of
cities and of temples, Sémiramis. In the 'Air de Sémiramis' of 1920,
her Sun-god calls Sémiramis to life at dawn: '"Existe! ... Sois enfin
toi-même!" dit l'Aurore' (o I, p 91). And later, in the 'mélodrame' of
1934, Sémiramis's extraordinary prayer – 'je me coucherai sur la
pierre de cet Autel, et je prierai le Soleil bientôt dans toute sa force,
qu'il me réduise en vapeur et en cendres' (o I, p 196) – is heard, and
her offered life changed into votive smoke on that mysterious altar
– 'L'Autel vide brille au soleil.'

In the following chiasmatic sentence, each of its two clauses stresses
the tension between surprise and newness on the one hand, and on
the other, the customary and 'déjà vu':

> Ne suis-je pas *accoutumé* à me *surprendre*,
>
> et *la nouveauté* n'est-elle pas ma sensation *la plus connue*?

'What would you be,' the magic Fay asks the dreaming Faust, 'without the unforeseen?':

> Que seriez-vous sans la surprise?
> L'esprit ne brille qu'il ne brise
> La ressemblance du passé...('Mon Faust,' o II, p 398).

The remainder of 'L'Unique' elaborates this paradox, which fascinated Valéry, and which was also brought out in the last of the three
'Réveils,' where the new, the unique ideas arose in the morning
mind, while the body resumed its customary routine: 'donc je vais, et

d'une part, je sens les Idées (très diverses) m'envahir, se disputer la
vie, etc. ... etc. ... mais d'autre part je me perçois allant et agissant en
plein automatisme...' That fragment also stressed the dichotomy of
mind and body which the present poem will develop near its close in
juxtaposing the *moi*'s 'esprit' with the beating of its heart.

One of the mind's laws, says the poet, is that it does not know itself,
fails to recognize its own cyclical functioning, part of nature's cycle:

> C'est peut-être la loi de l'esprit qu'il doive méconnaître la plus
> naïve de ses lois. Elle exige que le désir n'ait eu de pareil. Car le
> désir est tout puissance; mais le souvenir d'une puissance est im-
> puissance, et la force n'est que ma présence au plus haut point.

'Ma présence au plus haut point' echoes 'le plus haut de l'être' of
the preceding poem of the sequence; 'le désir est tout puissance' recalls 'la puissance qui est dans l'air avant l'orage.' Their very intensity
and virtual energy are due to the illusion of their uniqueness, thanks
to the mind's forgetfulness. It is in this that mind and body, 'connaître' and 'être,' are diametrically opposed. For the rhythmic repetition and return, the universal heartbeat of all life, is repugnant to
'l'esprit' in its eternal quest for the new. It is for this reason that
Valéry had no taste for the Vergilian bucolic, pastoral theme, as we
saw in discussing 'Moments.' The return of the seasons 'bores' him:
'La vie pastorale m'est étrangère et me semble ennuyeuse. ... Le
retour des saisons et de leurs effets donne l'idée de la sottise de
la nature et de la vie, laquelle ne sait que se répéter pour subsister'
(o I, p 208).

'La vie,' says Valéry in a *Cahier* entry, 's'oppose à l'intelligence
par sa forme périodique, l'intelligence est du type "une fois pour
toutes".' 'L'"esprit" (le plus esprit de l'esprit) répugne à la répétition. Résume – épuise – cherche la loi pour se débarrasser des
faits, du nombre, du prévu. Ce qui est prévu l'accable. Tout ce qui
recommence lui semble "bêtise," donc la "vie" ... Je t'ai vue et vécue
mille fois (Heure), car trois fois valent mille et dix mille pour Moi,
l'Esprit...'[8]

But Teste knows he is deluding himself when he prays: 'donnez ...
donnez la suprême pensée...' (o II, p 37). He knows that he cannot
reach beyond time, that the very life of his mind is made up of its
'returns.' A *Cahier* entry, entitled 'RE,' stresses the tension between the
mind's desire for uniqueness and its cyclical nature: '...l'organisme est
de cent façons obligé à des *retours* – recharges ou sommeils. Et ceci
domine son "temps." Et l'espèce se retrempe dans la mort des indivi-

dus combinée à la reproduction. Mais ceux qui *ont l'esprit* ont *de quoi ne pas* comprendre, ni accepter cette condition de leur existence et de celle de l'esprit' (c I, p 1093). And in another, entitled 'RE et SE-RE,' Valéry says: 'tout le fonctionnement mental dans les 3 domaines C E M est dominé par la reprise, répétition, recommencement, identité – ... Chaque instant est une combinaison que l'on *peut toujours* considérer *unique* et que l'on *doit toujours* reconnaître formée de parties reconnues' (c I, p 1074). In 'L'Unique' the tension between the spirit's aspiration for transcendence of, and its vital dependence on, Time, i.e., *Etre*, culminates in the final paragraph, which juxtaposes the mind's 'états exceptionnels' with the regular breathing and heartbeats that tie the self to the world:

> Mais, tandis que le moment même de l'esprit aspire à ce qui lui semble sans exemple, et que j'espère en des états exceptionnels, chaque battement de mon cœur redit, chaque souffle de ma bouche rappelle – que *la chose la plus importante est celle qui se répète le plus*.

In the third fragment of our sequence, 'Accueil du jour,' the persona finally steps out (of his matutinal reflections) into the real morning,

> Je fais un pas sur la terrasse...

the terrace serving as the stage of this *theatrum mundi*. At the same time, the divided self – 'le Toi et le Moi' – is both actor in and spectator of the performance:

> J'entre en scène dans mon regard.

The self is, then, both enclosed by the scene in which it performs and outside of the action which it beholds. And the tension of the whole poem will be that between these two selves, or between these two tendencies of oneself, of being a part, on the one hand, of the world's play – its opening act – and, on the other, of its transcendence: 'etre' and 'connaître.' So this third fragment is not merely sequentially related to the preceding one – the sun has now risen – but it resumes the theme that had emerged from 'L'Unique.'

The clash between *moi* and *monde*, the persona's anxiety and fear of being engulfed by and in the world, of being acted upon and becoming the passive object of space and time, ie, matter, pervades the second moment of the mind:

> Ma présence se sent l'égale et l'opposée de tout ce monde lumi-
> neux qui veut la convaincre qu'il l'environne. Voici le choc entier de
> la terre et du ciel. L'heure veut me saisir et le lieu croit m'enclore...

Again the image of the balance comes to mind, with 'ma présence' on
the one side, and 'tout ce monde' on the other, the former both 'equal'
and at the same time 'opposed' to the latter. We recall the same 'Moment,' when Man in his first encounter with the world both weighed
and was weighed by what he perceived: 'l'homme *pèse* ce qu'il *voit* et
en est *pesé*.' The third of the 'Réveils' suggested the same precarious
equilibrium of a moment when the *moi* felt itself both creator and
creature of '*ce qui est* – et ceci n'est que choc, stupeur, contraste.' There
also the clash of *moi* and *monde* is reflected by 'le choc entier de la
terre et du ciel.'

In 'Accueil du jour,' the persona is defending himself against the
world's temptations, a world personified with its progressive entice-
ments: 'ce monde ... qui *veut* [me] *convaincre* qu'il [m'] *environne*,'
'l'heure *veut* me *saisir*,' 'le lieu *croit* m'*enclore*.' 'Convaincre' suggests
'vaincre,' while the verbs 'environner,' 'saisir,' and 'enclore' threaten
to confine and imprison the self in that luminous morning scene it has
just entered. We have encountered the same anxiety, though less
acute, before in these morning pieces. In 'Notes d'aurore,' the soul,
'saisie d'une crainte, d'une tristesse, d'une tendresse qui l'opposent
encore à tant de puissance croissante, se tient un peu à l'écart, dans
une réserve inexprimable.' There, before giving in to life, giving itself
to feeling the world and letting itself be submerged in its being, the
self wavered, like dawn, between night and day. Again, the gnawing
worm, the Serpent of Knowledge hidden in the garden of Eden, comes
to mind, and his salute to Life: 'Grand Soleil, qui sonnes l'éveil/A
l'être, et de feux l'accompagnes,/Toi qui l'*enfermes* d'un sommeil/
Trompeusement peint de campagnes ... Toujours le mensonge m'a
plu/Que tu répands sur l'absolu,/O roi des ombres fait de flamme (o I,
p 139) [my italics]! The canker is in the rose, and the worm feeds on
the living, not on the dead:

> Le vrai rongeur, le ver irréfutable
> N'est point pour vous qui dormez sous la table,
> Il vit de vie, il ne me quitte pas ('Le Cimetière marin,' o I, p 150).

For there are two temptations enticing the self and threatening it with
annihilation: the world's splendor, that is the flesh, and that of the

very spirit, 'la tentation de l'esprit.' All of Valéry's major poems
reflect this tension between 'être' and 'connaître,' and Man torn
between these opposing forces, each one of which can be deadly.

The 'esprit' wants to transcend space and time, 'le site avec son
heure,' that 'monde' into and with which its 'corps' awakens, and
which gives it life:

> Mais le site avec son heure, ce n'est pour l'esprit qu'un incident – un
> événement – un démon comme un autre ... Tout ce jour, un
> démon de ma nuit personnelle.

The mind, however, cannot remain in its 'personal night' and will,
indeed, be conquered by the day. For 'CEM – le mon-corps, le mon-
esprit, le mon-monde,' we recall, 'sont 3 directions – qui se dessinent
toujours...' 'CEM ... cette considération des attributions est dans le
régime vie/connaissance – capitale. Ce régime opère continuelle-
ment entre ces *membres* qui sont, en quelque sorte, ses "trois-dimen-
sions"' (CI, pp 1147-8).

Vainly, says the persona, does the sun assault me, but vainly, also,
does he try to escape that light which he has entered, and which has
already extinguished his 'personal night':

> Vainement, le soleil m'obsède d'une immense image, merveilleuse-
> ment colorée, et me propose toutes les énigmes du visible ... Il y a
> bien d'autres offres en moi-même, qui ne sont de la terre ni des
> cieux.

For, miraculously, it is the very beauty of the young morning which
fills the mind and soul and makes up the substance – 'la matière' – of
the poem. None of those other profferings, 'qui ne sont de la terre ni
des cieux,' but precisely those of the earth and the sky arise with the
aubade:

> Tout ce beau jour si net, orné, borné de tuiles et de palmes, et de
> qui tant d'azur, accomplissant la plénitude, ferme dans le zenith la
> forme auguste, ne m'est qu'une bulle éphémère, pleine à demi
> d'objets indifférents.

This 'beautiful day,' *limited* by tiles and palms and *closed* at zenith –
'le plus haut de l'être' – and horizon, this mortal and 'ephemeral
bubble' of a day, is life. In the remainder of the poem, the poet paints
its 'objets indifférents' with love and passion. The drama of the mortal morning – 'on dirait que le jardin tremblant s'envole' ('Purs

Drames') – is rendered permanent in the poem's 'immense image, merveilleusement colorée.'

It is both a translucent bubble (viewed from without) and a globe of august form (from within), whose brilliant and vibrating luminosity, whose curved and flowing lines, are evoked by both the poem's signifiers and signified: 'ce beau jour ... orné, borné de tuiles et de palmes ... Bel Aujourd'hui ... tout ce qui brille et vibre.' Here rich internal rhymes and echoes, and the anagrammatic play of letters, fix the fleeting moment and transform *aube* into aubade, existence into the essence of image and song.

The poem's persona vainly tries to escape *that* day's – hoc die-hodie – fatal finality:

> bel *Aujourd'hui* que tu es – *Aujourd'hui* qui m'entoures – je suis *Hier* et *Demain* ... Tu n'es que ce qui est, et je ne suis jamais: je ne suis que ce qui peut être ... Ici, tout ce qui brille et vibre n'est pas moi.[9]

But 'entourer' resumes the closing-in movement of 'con-vaincre,' 'environner,' 'saisir,' and 'enclore' above. As dawn becomes day and its virtual forms realize themselves in their actuality, in existence, the familiar matutinal *moi* yearns nostalgically for that state of virtuality of 'Avant toute Chose.' In attempting to escape the here and now, the self would project itself beyond the existential, at once back into the past and forward into the future. Remembering dawns that have died and anticipating those yet to be born, it remains, of course, imprisoned in Time, and the plaything of Nature.

In the 'Note et digression,' Valéry states what he has expressed poetically in 'Accueil du jour': 'chaque personne étant un "jeu de la nature" ... les neuf dixièmes de sa durée se passent dans ce qui n'est pas encore, dans ce qui n'est plus, dans ce qui ne peut pas être; tellement que notre véritable *présent* a neuf chances sur dix de n'être jamais' (o i, pp 1227-8). He further discusses this paradox in 'La Politique de l'esprit,' where he points to the 'temporal,' ie, the 'human' experience of existence:

> une des plus extraordinaires inventions de l'humanité ... l'invention du *passé* et du *futur*. ... l'homme *créant le temps*, non seulement construit des perspectives en deçà et au delà de ses intervalles de réaction, mais, bien plus, *il ne vit que fort peu dans l'instant même*. Son établissement principal est dans le passé ou dans le futur. ... On peut dire de lui *qu'il lui manque indéfiniment ce qui n'existe pas* (o i, pp 1024-5).

The invention of Time marks the 'esprit's' differentiation from, and opposition to, Nature. Man, in living in the 'past' and 'future,' '...agit donc *contre nature, et son action est de celles qui opposent l'esprit à la vie.*' But in this 'opposition,' which we have encountered again and again in the aubades – which celebrate the privileged moment out of time and existence 'Avant toute Chose' – the mind's dependence on matter is repeatedly reaffirmed.

In the fragment's second part, we behold the persona advancing one step further into life and on the sunlit stage of the day:

> Je fais un pas de plus sur la terrasse...
> Je m'avance, comme un étranger, dans la lumière ... Quoi de plus étranger que celui qui se sent voir ce qu'il voit?

Here the day's bright splendour estranges the persona, who appears like an actor blinded by the stage lights. As he first 'goes on,' he is not yet 'in' his role, but sees himself playing it. He is both the 'persona' he plays, and at the same time a *moi* beholding himself playing his role. This image perfectly figures the familiar double self – 'et c'est le réveil. Le Toi et le Moi' – and the selves-consciousness of every *aube*: 'je me réveille,' 'je me lève,' 'je me vois,' 'je me parle' – 'je m'écris.'

The strange phenomenon of 'celui qui se sent voir ce qu'il voit' is the theme of the prose poem 'Sur la Place publique,' where the subject's successive retreats from itself, in order to behold itself as object, attain a limit beyond which it cannot recede. In that poem, the persona beholding a scene in the public square, a man feeding pigeons, observes himself observing that scene, thus creating a second spectacle and a second spectator, and as he tries one farther remove to make himself the observer of the one who observes himself, he reaches the mind's limit:

> Je me moque des pigeons. Je m'observe qui observe. J'écoute ce que me dit, ou ce que se dit, ce que je vois. ... Et ceci fait un second spectacle, qui se fait un second spectateur. Il m'engendre un témoin du second degré; et celui-ci est le *sumprême*. Il n'y a pas de troisième degré, et je ne suis pas capable de former quelque Quelqu'un qui voie *en deçà,* qui voie ce que fait et ce que voit celui qui voit *celui qui voit les pigeons.*
> Je suis donc à l'extrémité de quelque puissance; et il n'y a plus de place dans mon esprit pour un peu plus d'esprit (o ii, pp 688-9).

From the 'inside' (of his mind) our persona is now rejected and projected back to the 'outside,' into 'tout ce monde lumineux.' Its light now no longer merely 'proposes,' or offers the visible to him as before – 'le soleil ... me propose toutes les énigmes du visible' – but 'imposes,' ie, forces, its brilliance upon him. The *moi* is finally caught, 'fixed' and transfixed by the pure earth burning in the sun which it reflects:

> Le sol ardent et pur me fixe, et m'impose l'éclat de l'étendue de sa nudité.

Again the poet paints the image of this morning with rich alliterations and assonances, where big-bellied urns are heavy 'panses d'ombre,' and leaves sparkling in the sun nervous 'foyers de feuilles et de feux.' The silvery olive tree's vain attempts to brush off the pestering sparkles of *midi* light and heat reflect those of the self, imprisoned on that ground like tree and plant:

> Quelques vases, panses d'ombre, sont des foyers de feuilles et de feux. L'olivier sèchement se défend des étincelles qui l'irritent.

Even the birds are immobilized, as the sun gradually moves from morning to noon, that still-point of the world. The spirit is calm finally, conquered by the light of the day and the love of life:

> Sur un toit rose et blond dorment quatre colombes: je songe vaguement à la sensation de leur chair dans la plume douce et chaude posée sur l'argile tiède, ô Vie...

The perishable clay of which the world is made, and which will return to dust, is illuminated into a living radiance by the sun: 'un toit rose et blond,' and the *sensation* of the warm flesh of the doves sleeping in their soft, hot feathers on the baked clay, becomes that of all Life – which the persona apostrophizes and the poem so passionately celebrates. Elsewhere the poet exhorts the Spirit to strive not for immortal life, but to exhaust the realm of the living – and of the mortal:

> ...
> Beau ciel, vrai ciel, regarde-moi qui change!
> Après tant d'orgueil, après tant d'étrange
> Oisiveté, mais pleine de pouvoir,

Je m'abandonne à ce brillant espace,
Sur les maisons des morts mon ombre passe
Qui m'apprivoise à son frêle mouvoir.
...('La Cimetière marin,' o i, p 148).

The remainder of our fragment marks the 'falling off,' the *déchéance* from that moment of adoration and integration, the state of grace which the *moi* now rejects, and by which it is rejected. The poem's down-curve traces the necessary Fall after the cyclical matutinal elevation of the self – 'et à la moindre lueur, je rebâtis la hauteur d'où je tomberai ensuite.' We recall how, as the presence of Laure – 'l'or' – turned into memory, that morning poem became one of mourning. 'Le désir,' said the persona of 'L'Unique,' 'est toute puissance; mais le souvenir d'une puissance est impuissance.'

As another dawn turns into day, the *moi* disparages not merely all that lives in the world, 'tout ce pays' and 'toute la terre,' but also all that lives and dies in its mind:

Que m'importe tout ce pays? Que m'importe toute la terre? Mais que m'importe aussi tout ce qui vient à mon esprit, tout ce qui naît et meurt dans mon esprit?

This state recalls a similar one in one of the 'Réveils,' where the persona said 'la marque du réel, c'est l'insignifiance absolue.' And this attitude and exile, I remarked, is in this poetic universe depicted as the arid mountain – 'roches, neige, glaciers' – of the Solitary who has not merely left life behind him, but also no longer believes in 'l'idole Esprit.'

There are two forces courting the living: the world of matter and that of the mind: '*ce que je vois, ce que je pense.*' And the *moi*'s oscillation between these two, this very movement, constitutes its life:

Ce que je vois, ce que je pense – se disputent *ce que je suis.* Ils l'ignorent; ils le conduisent: ils le traitent comme une chose... Suis-je la chose d'une idée, et le jouet de la spendeur d'un jour?

The 'Moi pur' is but an Ideal fading away with the privileged moment of dawn; in 'real life,' the *moi* becomes a 'person,' and, as Valéry said in 'Note et digression,' 'chaque personne [est] un "jeu de la nature".'

The fourth and final of the 'Petits Poèmes abstraits' is not an aubade, but, on the contrary, a poem about nightfall. Valéry wrote few

evening prose poems, and 'La Rentrée' appears as a fixed piece closing off this sequence, rather than a characteristic free and mobile
fragment.[10] Its tone of appeasement contrasts with the tone of the preceding poems of the sequence, and the familiar singular *moi*-persona
is hidden here in an unfamiliar plural voice:

> Revenons ... L'or se meurt, et toute chose peu à peu se fonce et se
> dégrade. Le sol fume. Un diamant déjà perce dans l'altitude.

The world's gentle death – 'Laure se meurt' – is invoked in a tone of
condolence and consolation and, therefore, evokes the presence of
another. All the forms of life, which we have again and again seen
emerge at dawn, gradually merge and are submerged – 's'amassent,'
'se confondent' – in that 'profonde unité des ténèbres' which decomposes them like death:

> Les demeures et les domes de feuilles s'amassent et se confondent; et
> toute la variété de la figure de la terre insensiblement s'assemble et
> se compose en un seul troupeau de formes vagues et obscures accablé
> de torpeur. Autour de nous, bientôt, la profonde unité des
> ténèbres sera.[11]

The 'troupeau de formes vagues et obscures accablé de torpeur,' evocative of the shades of Hades rather than a world asleep, confounds
the human and the non-human, rendered equal and inanimate all, by
death.
    The purest – *la lumière* – has left the earth and rises up to form the
starry universe. Thus the divine divides itself from the human and its
time, all of whose weight bows *our* silent heads:

> Le plus pur de ce qui existe, le plus pur *nous* laisse et s'élève. Le
> haut ciel lentement se déclare univers. Quelque divinité se divise du
> temps, et tout le poids d'un jour de *notre* vie *nous* fait baisser la tête.
> Le silence *nous* prend: il *nous* sépare, il *nous* unit. Une est la lassitude
> [my italics].

While dawn's elevation is always unique and that of an unequaled
moi, the oncoming night's weariness is shared among men. Valéry
also elaborated the communal observation of the end of a day in the
prose poem 'Un Phénomène' from the sequence 'Mers,' where he
describes the effects of a sunset:

Coucher du soleil. Ciel pur, le disque orange est tangent à l'horizon.
Les personnages qui sont sur la plage se taisent sans savoir pourquoi. Silence de trois minutes.
Impression de solennité de ce passage. Il y a une sensation d'exécution capitale dans la profondeur implicite de cette durée. La tête de ce jour lentement tombe.
Le disque est bu. Quand il disparaît net, un enfant crie: *Ça y est!* Chacun semble frappé d'avoir vu *l'un de ses jours décapité devant soi* (o II, p 664).[12]

In our sequence, morning's life-creative thought – 'l'idée qui vient crée un homme nouveau' – has now become 'sad shadows of thoughts,' the simplest, the grandest, the vain, and the bitter, confounded all, like 'la variété de la figure de la terre,' in the general night. And under the cover of darkness myths emerge, where once was lucidity and light:

Les tristes ombres des plus simples, des plus grandes, des plus amères et vaines ou naïves pensées nous accompagnent. A la faveur du soir, les mythes viennent, et se font plus sensibles et importantes que toutes choses.

In the following paragraph 'Revenons' echoes the poem's opening, but now the collective 'nous' becomes a 'you and I,' the persona and his beloved, a silent presence to whom the remainder of the fragment is addressed. For all the terrors of the hour will henceforth be projected into the other, the woman. In one of the 'Aphorismes' of *Mélange*, Valéry said: 'La fin du jour est femme' (o I, p 303).[13]
The persona beseeches his companion to return, to hurry back from all that threatens outside to the protective light and warmth inside:

Revenons ... Recourons à la flamme et aux lampes. Asseyez-vous auprès de moi. Vos mains froides, vos pieds mouillés tendus a la braise, vos yeux songent des étincelles. La vie et la mort dansent et craquent devant vous.

The *moi* becomes her protector, and the witness – 'je sais bien, toutefois,' 'je sais, en toute certitude,' 'je ... ressens comme si j'étais dans votre chair' – of her fears:

Je sais bien, toutefois, que vous sentez et présumez en vous-même la présence de tous les ennemis de notre vie. *Ce qui ne sera plus, ce qui*

> *sera*, voilà l'une et l'autre puissance. Et c'est pourquoi vous frissonez
> devant la flamme furieuse, et vous êtes faible et contrainte, toute
> réduite à votre cœur serré, muette et lamentable au sein des
> formes du bonheur.

Thus the weakness and constraint, the heavy-heartedness and the
pitifulness of man alone in the night is rejected by the *moi* which
attributes them to the other, or to that other part of the self – which is
woman. In one of the 'Aperçus' of *Mélange*, Valéry says: 'Tout
homme contient une femme. Mais jamais sultane mieux cachée que
celle-ci' (o i, p 387).

The fundamental oneness of these two sides of the self – the male
'esprit' and the female 'âme' of the aubades – is finally symbolized,
on the narrative level, by the protective embrace which shields both
lover and beloved from the threats of night and death:

> Une personne est bien peu de chose auprès tant de périls qui
> émanent d'elle, la nuit venue. Je le ressens comme si j'étais dans
> votre chair. C'est pourquoi il faut se prendre dans les bras l'un de
> l'autre, et les paupières fortement fermées, étreindre une chose
> vivante, et se cacher dans une existence.

11 'Méditation avant pensée'

Méditation avant pensée' is the first sequence (o ı, pp 351-2) of the 'Poésie brute' section of *Mélange*, and the first of its three numbered pieces is, as mentioned in the preceding chapter, the opening, 'Avant toute Chose,' of the 'Petits Poèmes abstraits.' From its appearance there in 1932 to its reappearance here in 1939, the mobile fragment remained unchanged except for the omission of its title, which in slightly altered form became that of the new sequence.[1]

The two titles, moreover, are essentially synonymous, as they both designate the same moment of the matutinal *moi*, when the mind is in that ideal 'Zéro' state of pure potentiality, 'qui en précède toutes les pensées particulières,' and when the soul 'jouit de sa lumière sans objets' – before all things, and before all thoughts. The opening fragment of our sequence is not merely much longer than the other two, but it is also the only one which is a characteristic morning piece, while ıı and ııı constitute two brief, and more general, meditations on the functioning of the mind and consciousness.

We recall that 'Avant toute Chose' celebrated the first moment of the self and its day, 'un moment premier de proposition,' when the soul was still 'également éloigné de tous les noms et de toutes les formes.' The aubade captured again, but uniquely, the transient moment before the world takes shape, before the universal self – 'sur le plus haut de l'être' – becomes a person, a mere secular detail and congeries of miserable cares outside the privileged moment – 'ô moment, diamant du Temps...' And the subsequent poems of the preceding sequence then developed the spirit's attempts to transcend time, as well as its ultimate resignation to, and acceptance of, life and *Vergänglichkeit*, of mortality.

The second fragment of 'Méditation avant pensée' likewise deplores the falling off from that former state of grace, of purity and

absence, which Valéry elsewhere described as 'le sans-attribut, ni
image, ni valeur du "moi pur",' that of the 'Zéro mathématique' of
the mind which we have discussed. Our persona apostrophizes consciousness and laments its promiscuity:

> O conscience! A laquelle il faut toujours et toujours des événe-
> ments! Il suffit que tu sois pour être remplie.

This fragment, we have noted, is not strictly speaking an aubade, but a
little meditation on the mind in general, no longer in its ideal state,
but in its ordinary and customary everyday functioning, with all its
contingencies and inconstancies, its impurity. The daily wretched
mental prostitution and debasement which our persona bemoans recalls Diderot's *Neveu de Rameau*, whose 'lui'-*moi* dialoguing with
himself – 'je m'entretiens avec moi-même' – admits: 'j'abandonne
mon esprit à tout son libertinage ... mes pensées sont mes catins.'[2]
And the awakening persona of 'Aurore' scolds his ideas in no gentler
terms:

> Quoi! c'est vous, mal déridées!
> Que fites-vous, cette nuit,
> Maîtresses de l'âme, Idées,
> Courtisanes par ennui (o I, p 112)!

Valéry examines the functioning of the mind, its cyclical progres-
sions and the haphazard production and destruction of its thoughts,
throughout the *Cahiers*, and also as 'la matière' of some of his prose
poems. Her changing states of mind and consciousness, for example,
are the main theme of 'Agathe,' who beholds her ideas rise apparently
'sans commencement' and disappear just as mysteriously. We recall,
moreover, how 'L'Amateur de poèmes' deplores the fortuitous
nature of thought, its lack of order:

> Si je regarde tout à coup ma véritable pensée, je ne me console pas
> de devoir subir cette parole intérieure sans personne et sans origine;
> ces figures éphémères; et cette infinité d'entreprises interrom-
> pues par leur propre facilité, qui se transforment l'une dans l'autre,
> sans que rien ne change avec elles. Incohérente sans le paraître,
> nulle instantanément comme elle est spontanée, la pensée, par sa
> nature manque de style (o I, p 94).

The ideal 'vide' and 'la pureté du Non-être' are seen as opposed to life, to that life in which the self must immerse itself each day anew:

> Toujours, tu préfères le hasard au vide, et le chaos au rien.
> Tu es faite pour toute chose, et tu te fais n'importe quelle chose pour ta substitution infinie.

For Valéry the origin of all thought, as noted in the discussion of 'Reprise,' is pure chance: 'il ne faut jamais oublier que nos pensées sont uniquement portées et développées par les *occasions*. L'accident est ce qu'il y a de plus constant.' 'Toute puissance spirituelle est fondée sur les innombrables hasards de la pensée' (c I, pp 251, 924). And the infinite substitutions of the mind, of consciousness, its disorder and chaos – out of which the poet creates order and his poetic cosmos – were in part the subject matter of the *Cours de poétique*: 'le fond de la pensée est toujours désordre, chaos, d'images, de mots, d'impulsions, de schèmes qui se forment et se déforment.'

Consciousness is fickle; it will run off with any of its prevailing chimaeras or fabrications, its monsters of the moment:

> Et quel monstre que tu fasses, tu ne veux pas l'avoir vu en vain.
> Invinciblement aussi, tu te divises, et t'attaches à une de tes parties: tel fantôme sera le vainqueur des autres; telle parole, la plus puissante; telle idée plus étendue que son lieu, plus durable que son instant. Pourquoi? – Adieu.

The mind, then, forever questing for adventure, will become the slave of its current 'idée fixe,' its Master Notion, which sings triumphantly:

> Je suis venue comme un hasard dans l'agitation de ta tête.
> Mais toi, d'autres hasards et une autre face des choses
> T'ont fait comme pour moi.
> En route! En chasse! Cours après qui t'anime (o I, p 358)!

These love affairs of the mind are like all others: each new adventure and infatuation is unique. At the end of her night, the persona of 'Agathe,' that 'poème de l'intellect,' knows that the chance encounter of her mind and its idea can become the passing, but consuming, passion of a moment:

> Une [idée] se lève d'elle-même, et se met à la place d'une autre;
> nulle d'entre elles ne peut être plus importante que son heure. Elles
> montent, originales; dans un ordre insensé; mystérieusement mues
> jusque vers le midi admirable de ma présence, *où brûle, telle qu'elle
> est, la seule chose qui existe; l'une quelconque* (o II, p 1392) [my italics].

Since time immemorial poets have celebrated love without understanding its mystery. The mind's passions are as inexplicable as any
others; our fragment's closing 'Pourquoi?' remains unanswered.

The third fragment of our sequence further develops this meditation on the mind, its *gourmandise* at once destructive and constructive.
The poet here ascribes to 'l'esprit' those natural impulses usually not
associated with the mind, and the most fundamental of physical
drives: hunger, 'l'instinct de dévorer,' which is then further stressed
with 'digérer':

> L'instinct de dévorer, d'épuiser, de résumer, d'exprimer une fois
> pour toutes, d'en finir, de digérer définitivement les choses, le
> temps, les songes, de tout ruiner par la prévision, de chercher par là
> autre chose que les choses, le temps, et les songes, c'est là l'instinct
> extravagant et mystérieux de l'esprit.

The mind feeds on the world as does the organism, consumes and
transforms its raw material into its own substance. This nutrition
metaphor, moreover, recalls that other fragment, in which the 'hungry' mind was likened to the tiger about to attack his prey:

> Il est des instants (vers l'aube) où mon esprit ... se sent cet appétit
> essentiel et universel qu'il oppose au Tout comme un tigre à un trou-
> peau; mais aussi une sorte de malaise: celui de ne savoir à quoi s'en
> prendre et quelle proie particulière saisir et attaquer (o II, p 1532).

The mind in consuming the world reduces it to its own matter; it
makes, in fact, a 'World' out of the indeterminate manifold which
feeds it:

> Rien que le mot: Monde, en est un indice évident.

And like Caracalla, it wants to have done with it once and for all, 'une
fois pour toutes,' and all at once:

C'est toujours Caracalla qui souhaitait une seule tête à couper.

Nihilisme laborieux, qui ne juge avoir bien détruit que ce qu'il a pénétré, mais qui ne peut bien comprendre que dans la mesure où il a su construire. Nihilisme bizarrement constructeur ... Mais il s'agit de refuser ce que l'on peut: mais ce pouvoir doit d'abord être acquis et vérifié.

In Meditations II and III Valéry, in associating the mental and the libidinal, 'l'esprit' with hunger and sex, suggests again the fundamental interdependence of *corps*, *esprit* and *monde*, 'C E M.' At the same time, the tension created by the hungry mind wanting both to feed on and transcend its body and its world is again marked by its refusal: 'mais il s'agit de refuser ce que l'on peut.' This hunger-strike of the spirit, its threatened and threatening refusal to eat, recalls 'Accueil du jour' and the *moi*'s refusal to enter the day, that is life: 'il y a bien d'autres offres en moi-même, qui ne sont de la terre ni des cieux.' That same renouncement was voiced in the 'tiger' fragment:

chaque objet particulier lui paraît [à l'esprit] devoir diminuer, s'il s'y attache, *la sensation divine* de son groupe *de puissance* éveillé, et il pressent dans tout le jour qui va suivre une incarnation, et donc une réduction de *cette illusion du pouvoir à l'état pur*; que son sens intime place au-dessus de tout [my italics].[3]

The 'Moi pur,' that 'divine' self, is paradoxically an ideal that is part *as such* of human reality: and the mind must both transcend and feed on the world which it at once destroys and reconstructs.

12 'La Considération matinale'

The short fragment, 'La Considération matinale,' is again mobile within the œuvre, appearing twice, with very minor variants, in Mauvaises Pensées et autres (o II, pp 808-9, 879) of 1941.[1] It had already appeared, moreover, as part of the sequence 'Matines,' which Valéry published in 1938 in the Cahiers du Sud.[2]

This particular 'Considération' lacks the high intensity of the unique, first person-persona's presence, as well as the expansion created by the co-naissance of the world with and in this consciousness, which we know from other aubades. It is, rather, that of an anonymous voice reflecting upon the awakening mind in general:

> L'être, au réveil, tout au percé du jour, est encore très peu ce qu'il va être par son nom et le reflux de sa mémoire.

Though the hyperbolic 'MOI' appears twice in the fragment, it is 'son MOI' and 'ce MOI' and not the familiar 'My-Self' as the soul of the awakening world. It is, in fact, hardly a self at all:

> Il est à peine soi; mais son MOI naturel, universel, assez simple encore pour ressentir, pour traiter également, et même équitablement, toutes choses.

This self, which treats the world's 'choses' equally and justly, appears, then, not merely 'before all things,' but 'outside' that world and has the distance and impersonality of a God, as well as a 'judging' God's justice:

> Il est encore avant son inégalité particulière acquise et apprise; il est encore en dehors du monde, non engagé, non partie, mais juge pur.

The self here no longer rises with and to the Sun, but wants to become that Sun itself – 'ce Soleil monte comme un juge' – but, unlike the Sun, it does not embrace the world to give it life.

It is another dimension, that of suffering and, above all, that of desire – 'Toute l'âme s'appareille/A l'extrême du désir...' – which raises the human to the divine and creates a God within the self. The matutinal *moi*'s exultation, its 'lucidité douloureuse' and its 'amour et soif et point de nom' makes poems out of thoughts, aubades of *aubes*, and psalms out of dawns. In both *Mauvaises Pensées et autres* and the 'Matines' sequence of the *Cahiers du Sud* our 'Considération matinale' is followed by a:

> Petit Psaume du Matin
> Mon esprit pense à mon esprit.
> Mon histoire m'est étrangère.
> Mon nom m'étonne et mon corps est idée.
> Ce que je fus est avec tous les autres.
> Et je ne suis même pas ce que je vais être.

13 'A Grasse'

'A Grasse,' a sequence of three numbered pieces, is from *Mélange* (o I, pp 291-3); its first and second fragments appeared in a 1927 *Cahier* (c II, pp 1285-6), while the third fragment in free verse had appeared already in that form, though with minor variants in blocking, in a 1935 *Cahier* (c II, pp 1298-9).[1]

The opening poem awakens to the sounds and scents of a dawn in which the worlds of nature and of man are in harmony, as bells and birds and frogs sing in the morning, where human industry distills flowers into their perfumed quintessence:

> Cloches tintent;
>   Grenouilles croassent et ciseaux gazouillent
>   Croassements reguliers comme une scie, et sur ce fond, tout le cisaillement pépié des oiseaux.
>   Odeurs. On ne sait si ce sont les jardins qui les émanent ou les fabriques de parfums.

The piece thus reconciles town and country in one of the poet's oft-poetized cities, Grasse, whose anagram is hidden in the poem's second line, while its 'surface' celebrates croaking frogs and warbling birds:

> Grenouilles croassent et ciseaux gazouillent.[2]

This line, with its anagrammatic play of letters, its alliterations and internal rhymes, demonstrates again Valéry's virtuosity as an accomplished composer of the sound-look of letters, of words, of the poetry of prose. In this the line reflects, of course, the fragment and the entire sequence, the whole of which it is an organic part.

I have mentioned that Valéry wrote a substantial group of prose poems about cities he loved; and he frequently painted these in their awakening at dawn, as in the fragment 'Nice,' discussed above.

An essential part of the world's diurnal rebirth is its morning birds, the 'oiseaux premiers,' their 'pluralité vivante au plus haut des cieux.' In that fragment, as in the present one, their little cries become 'chips and chisels,' likened to scissor cuttings – 'menus coups de ciseaux,' 'le cisaillement pépié des oiseaux' – in and of dawn's silence: 'quel silence à découdre!'[3] The sound-image of scissors cutting into silence is reinforced in our fragment with the frogs' 'sawing': 'croassements réguliers comme une scie.'

From morning's sounds the poem progresses to its scents, the smells of flower gardens and of the perfume industry of Grasse, to prepare for the second fragment, which celebrates the sense of sight: '*Je vois* de ma fenêtre au centre de *ma vue...*'

From '*on* ne sait' we pass to '*je* vois,' and this *moi* becomes an eye, as in 'Purs Drames,' beholding the morning world unfolding outside the window. But while the 'oeil pur' of the early prose poem reflected a Symbolist garden, whose sole human presence was the mythic First Couple, the mature artistic vision perceives and conceives the 'real' world – 'ceci est France' – and at its centre a man who tills his field:

> Je vois de ma fenêtre au centre de ma vue un homme qui pioche son champ. Il avance pas à pas dans sa tâche, courbé, planté, par ses deux jambes en terre – chemise blanche et pantalon bleu – il pioche, et puis met les mains dans la terre.

The matutinal *moi*-persona of our aubade is no longer turned inward and self-reflective, but reflects the young day outside. He literally 'abandons himself' to the world to which he belongs by his body and which he beholds through the eye, a world which, in turn, becomes meaningful in and through this human consciousness. Thus *mon-corps*, *mon-esprit*, and *mon-monde* are now balanced in a harmonious equilibrium, as the *moi* embraces life, and thus mortality, which it shares with all men. Both the cycle of nature, with its births and deaths, and Man's participation in it, are mirrored in the poem's image of the man toiling in the earth, 'planté par *ses deux jambes en terre*,' '*puis il met les mains dans la terre*' [my italics].

The motif of human industry which will grow into one of the poem's major themes, that of *Homo-Faber* evoked above with 'les fabriques,' is now taken up with 'il avance pas à pas dans sa tâche, courbé,' to be developed further on with 'il travaille, il y a des

hommes qui ont besoin de ce qu'il fait là.' And it will culminate in
the fragment's last paragraph, which celebrates 'l'homme – machine
adaptée.'

This is the only aubade con-centrating on Man at the centre of the
world – 'au centre de ma vue est un homme qui pioche,' 'il est au
centre du pays que je vois' – a world marked everywhere by his presence, from the city's morning bells, the houses in the countryside to
the olive trees, the very symbol of human agri-culture since antiquity:

> Il est au centre du pays que je vois qui s'élargit autour de lui,
> s'élève de crête en crête jusqu'aux montagnes, de vague blonde
> en vague bleue, porteur de maisons claires toutes petites, de troupes
> d'oliviers, de pointes noires qui sont des cyprès.

The image of the concentric waves of the landscape rising around its
human centre, 'autour de lui,' is reflected in the harmonious rhythms,
's'élève de crête en crête,' and the gentle flow, 'de vague blonde
en vague bleu' of the signifiers. And in celebrating *la terre* the poet
thus suggests *la mer*, land and water, *fons et origo* of all life.

In embracing life and 'the realm of the possible,' the *moi* shares it
with all things mortal, and with his fellow man:

> Voici encore un paysan qui épuce ses roses, cambré en bras de
> chemise, au milieu d'oiseaux qui lui partent sous le nez, et vont tom-
> ber sur la cime ou sur la branche avancée du cerisier.

The peasant tending his flowers cultivates matter to extract from it an
ideal essence, the fragrance and the form, the colour and the texture of
the rose. In a like manner, the awakening mind again and again
creates an ideal order and cosmos out of chaos, and the poet in weav-
ing his text draws a poem out of a dawn.

In this aubade, dawn's familiar hues celebrate human architecture
in the 'maison en forme de temple fermé' amidst the olive trees, with
its gently sloped roof, its tiles lighting up in the sun, and its gables and
shutters:

> Douceur de la couleur et de la figure de cette maison en forme de temple
> fermé au milieu des oliviers; cela est d'une chaux dédorée où le
> rose de l'aurore, l'ocre, le laiteux se mêlent; le toit aux pentes douces
> couvert de tuiles tachées de rouille et de tan, le triangle bas des pig-
> nons, les volets gris et bleuâtres, les groupes de trois cyprès massifs.

I have mentioned that for Valéry architecture is the realization of creative thought in *œuvre* par excellence. For it is characterized by utility as well as beauty, by solidity and duration, those qualities which the Phèdre of 'Eupalinos ou l'architecte' calls 'les grands caractères d'une oeuvre complète.' In that Dialogue, Socrates affirms: 'la seule *architecture* les exige, et les porte au plus haut point,' whereupon Phèdre declares: 'je la regarde comme le plus complet des arts' (o II, p 130).

The harmonious architectural lines revealed by our poem's dawn are reflected in the texture of the text, with its echoes and alliterations: 'douceur de la couleur,' 'la figure de cette maison en forme fermée au milieu des oliviers,' 'tuiles tachées de rouille et de tan.' Even the trees surrounding the edifice, 'les groupes de trois cyprès massifs,' harmonize with its lines, 'le triangle bas des pignons.'

The celebration of the morning sun's gold awakening the house's 'forme fermée,' 'une chaux dédorée' in the 'rose de l'aurore,' recalls Eupalinos's temple, 'ce temple [qui] est l'image mathématique d'une fille de Corinthe, que j'ai heureusement aimée' (o II, p 92), as well as the columns 'si froides et dorées' of the 'Cantique des colonnes':

> Filles des nombres d'or,
> Fortes des lois du ciel,
> Sur nous tombe et s'endort
> Un dieu couleur de miel.

The brief phrase:

> Naguère, elle était à Maeterlinck

connects the house with its former owner, the Belgian poet and dramatist, thus linking architecture and poetry. For poetry, like the other art, constructs and composes. Again in 'Eupalinos,' Socrates says:

> mais véritablement, la parole peut construire comme elle peut créer, comme elle peut corrompre ... je lui donnerais trois visages: l'un, presque informe, signifierait la parole commune: celle qui meurt à peine née ... mais le second visage jetterait par sa bouche arrondie, un flot cristallin d'eau éternelle: il aurait les traits les plus nobles, l'oeil grand et enthousiaste; le col puissant et gonflé, que les statuaires donnent aux Muses.

Phèdre:

> Et le troisième?

Socrate:

> Il y faudrait je ne sais quelle physionomie inhumaine, avec des traits de cette rigueur et de cette subtilité qu'on dit que les Egyptiens ont su mettre sur le visage de leurs dieux.

And he continues:

> nous bâtissons, pareils à Orphée, au moyen de la parole, des temples de sagesse et de science ... Ce grand art exige de nous un langage admirablement exact ... Car, qu'est-ce, la raison, sinon le discours lui-même? ... Il faut donc ajuster ces paroles complexes comme des blocs irréguliers, spéculant sur les chances et les surprises que les arrangements de cette sorte nous réservent, et donner le nom de "poètes" à ceux que la fortune favorise dans ce travail (o II, pp 111-13).

The middle fragment of our sequence already foreshadows, with its celebration of architecture, the final one, which constitutes the perfect poetic structure and construction of a dawn rising, like the world, to Orpheus's lyre. Both architecture and poetry, however, are first once again linked to the peasant cultivating the earth, the founder of all civilization and its arts:

> L'homme qui pioche – machine adaptée – les pieds bien plantés dans l'épaisseur de la terre; mais il frappe, et il y a le gros effort de retirer le fer, puis de redresser le corps et la tête, autour de la ceinture, hisser la masse du torse, et encore, et encore. Le silence et le souffle de cet homme qui peine.[4]

The culminating fragment of 'A Grasse' is in *vers libre*; we have already encountered this phenomenon of a prose poem passing into this rhythmic form.[5] Though our study is limited to Valéry's prose aubades, it must include 'A Grasse III' as it constitutes an integral – even the culminating – part of this sequence, although it had been written, as noted, separately, and already in free verse, in a 1935 *Cahier*. For this italicized *vers libre* aubade marks the poem proper, that is the poet's 'product' in a sequence celebrating human industry.

Valéry frequently referred to poetry as a 'literary product' pro-
duced or 'fabricated' for a market of 'consumers,' thus linking literature to the other arts and artifacts and their economy. In the
'Première Leçon du Cours de Poétique,' for example, in undertak-
ing 'l'exploration du domaine de l'esprit créateur,' he borrows
'quelques mots à l'Economie':

> il me sera peut-être commode d'assembler sous les seuls noms de
> *production* et de *producteur*, les diverses activités et les diverses per-
> sonnages dont nous aurons à nous occuper ... Il ne sera pas moins
> commode ... que l'on parle du lecteur sous le nom économique de
> *consommateur*. ... Sans insister sur ma comparaison économique, il est
> clair que l'idée de travail, les idées de création et d'accumulation
> de richesse, d'offre et de demande, se présentent très naturellement
> dans le domaine qui nous intéresse (o I, p 1344).

And in 'Poésie et pensée abstraite,' the poet likens the poem to a
machine: 'En vérité, un poème est une sorte de machine à produire l'état poétique au moyen des mots' (o I, p 1337). Valéry moreover stresses repeatedly how much his work, and how much of his
work is the product of demand. The *ego scriptor* says: 'D'ailleurs le
destin a voulu que je sois toute ma vie l'escalve du sujet imposé.
(Toute ma prose! moins ces notes.)' (c I, p 290).[6]
    In our culminating fragment, we behold the world rising toward
the sun, which is behind the persona, a *moi* who becomes 'mes yeux.'
His become our eyes, as his presence is entirely effaced by his discourse, this pure poem to dawn:

> *Au milieu de la campagne sombre encore*
> *Une maison se dore et un amandier en fleurs, seul,*
> *S'illumine – démontrant le soleil à mes yeux*
> *Qui ne le voient pas directement;*

As the persona's eyes see the morning sun not directly, but reflected
in the *paysage*, we see the golden springtime morning reflected in a
text abounding, again, in internal echoes and alliterations. And the
aubade celebrating this *aurore* contains the latter's anagram in its first
line, so that the poem's very opening is literally – by the letters –
embraced by daybreak's double gold /or/-/or/:

> *Au milieu de la campagne sombre encore*

This gold is then echoed in 'une maison se dore,' 'un
amandier ... s'illumine,' to be taken up again with 'un grand
Arbre ... s'enflamme';

> Et un grand Arbre, d'entre les arbres et les plantes obscures,
> S'enflamme, secouant dans le vent froid du matin
> Toute une foule de groupes
> Tout un désordre de détails délicats,
> De sa masse lumineuse de verdure.
> Les oliviers à leur tour naissent à leur figure fine
> Et brouillée d'argent;
> La Rose fade de l'Arbre de Judée se montre.

This aubade abounds in trees: the blossoming almond tree, the
'grand Arbre d'entre les arbres,' the olive trees, the Judas tree, and
further on 'les masses de pins crépues.' The major Valéryan theme
of the tree has been studied; its presence in our poem confers upon
this dawn its familiar double tension.[7] For the tree's roots sink as
deeply into the dark earth as its golden crown rises into the light, so
that the landscape's tree-tops glowing in the morning sun remind us
of the obscure underside of this young world. But the tree represents
also another tension: that of multiplicity in unity, the fragment's autonomy and, at the same time, its organic relationship to the whole of
which it constitutes an integral part. The big Tree's 'désordre de
détails délicats' makes up its 'masse lumineuse de verdure.' And in
this the Tree reflects this dawn made up of its infinite fragments
gradually revealed by the rising sun – 'Chaque partie se subdivise./
Chaque fragment peut vivre de sa forme.' – which come together to
form one world.

The predominance of reflexive verbs in the text – 'se dore,'
's'illumine,' 's'enflamme,' 's'accusent,' 'se précise,' 'se subdivise,' 'se
fait' – culminating in the fivefold repetition of 'se montre,' stresses the
seemingly independent autogenesis of each of the fragments, the diverse phenomena of dawn, and at the same time recalls their role as
passive reflectors of the life-giving light. As the sun rises higher on the
horizon, the constituent components of the world come into existence
and into view in an ascending rhythm created by the accumulation of
very short sentences. This acceleration reaches its highest intensity in
a kind of litany:

> La Rose fade de l'Arbre de Judée se montre.
> Le toit rouge de tuiles se montre.

> *Les masses de pins crépues se montrent.*
> *Les formes de collines se montrent.*
> *Tout se montre, avec de fortes ombres qui s'accusent.*

The progression is from the smaller, the rose, to the larger, the roof, masses of trees, hills, to the 'tout se montre,' in a passage recalling the dawn of the 'Dialogue de l'arbre': 'Tendrement naît l'aurore, et toute chose se déclare. Chacune dit son nom, car le feu du jour neuf la réveille à son tour' (o II, p 178). There, as in this poem and all of these aubades, the present tense of the verbs recreates a unique *aube* in all its immediacy, an immediacy further heightened in our poem by the absence of the intermediary persona; he, as we have noted, is effaced by the discourse.

When he reappears in the text with 'je distingue chaque feuille' and 'je puis séparer chaque objet,' dawn has already risen and accomplished itself:

> *Les noms se sont posés définitivement sur les choses.*

Yet this aubade celebrating the reconciliation of the self with the world, the *moi*'s acceptance of life and mortality ('il faut tenter de vivre!') which I have chosen as the culminating sequence of our discussion, remains open-ended:

> *Ce qui va être se débrouille et se dégage...*

The fragment, as well as the sequence, remains 'open' in the manner of the entire cycle of dawn prose poems, these 'reprises' and successive approximations, 'l'infini des approximations successives,' which are arrested or 'closed' only by the poet's death.

14 Conclusion

In my reading of Valéry's prose aubades, my immediate aim has not been a study of the theme of dawn in the poet's work, though that has necessarily emerged from the discussion. Rather, I have chosen primarily to examine the poet's artistic strategy in a representative group of prose poems related in both subject and manner. Their characteristic manner, or form, is that of the poetic prose fragment which, as we have seen, is frequently a mobile structural element of the characteristic Valéryan 'sequence.' I have noted the recent critical interest in the break-up of traditional literary genres, and have remarked that Valéry's decisive position in this development has so far been generally neglected. Yet we find in Valéry's artistic progression from the traditional prose poem to the fragment, the evolution of the *recueil* to the sequence, a phenomenon very similar to that manifest in another new prose form, the new *nouveau roman*, which Jean Thibaudeau describes in terms that could well apply to our prose aubades:

> A mesure que le texte s'éloigne du statut de *brouillon*, manuscrit, indéfini, pour se ranger à celui de publication, imprimée, finie ses "fragments" deviennent des "séquences."
>
> *Fragments*: où la recherche d'une formulation définitive, en chacun, tend à mettre à sa suite, à emporter dans son mouvement et à sa guise l'ensemble des fragments. Lesquels sont comme les vestiges d'un livre cependant futur, livre qui serait un *ailleurs* mythologiquement tangible, espace écrit-sonore, indéfiniment riche et infiniment désirable, livre-futur-déjà-écrit à quoi se réfère sans doute le projet romanesque.
>
> *Séquence*: où la recherche d'une formulation définitive tend à mettre chacune à une place relative, *ici*, dans le cours de ce roman en voie d'achèvement.

> Le fragment veut être le début de toute parole et son éternité.
> La séquence devrait être (si elle est réussie) l'efficace du début,
> à sa manière, en tel point ou moment d'un texte, écrit, qui sans
> cesse recommence.[1]

We have found, moreover, that these dawn fragments and sequences, the prose aubades, involve us in a great number of Valéry's major themes, from anguish to art, from language to love, from birth to death. For from both thematic and structural points of view, any one aspect is necessarily a part of the whole, one single theme but a fragment of a universe in which all themes are dynamically and organically interrelated. It has been my aim to show the vital interrelationship of these poetic prose fragments with the corpus of Valéry's poetry, as well as that of the theme of dawn with the others with which it forms an ideational and ideological cosmos. And the interrelationship of *forme* and *fond*, of the theme and its expression, is such in this poetry that the one engaged us necessarily and simultaneously in the other; thus, for example, one of Valéry's brief reflections on the exchange between 'je' and 'moi' upon awakening was shaped into a miniature matutinal dialogue (cf. 'Fragments'); and 'Purs Drames' (cf. chapter devoted to that poem), a poem about a mythic Eden, took on the language and the form of a fable.[2]

Before briefly retracing some of the major themes encountered in these aubades, I should like to recall certain features which almost all of them share. I observed at the outset of this study that these poems are almost all mono-dialogues of the self with itself as it rediscovers its body and mind and the world, when *mon-corps, mon-esprit*, and *mon-monde* come together to form the beginning of a new day. Each aubade, therefore, has a first-person persona that frequently doubles into 'I' and 'me'; who sometimes is a poet-persona; and the poems are all in the present tense. For as the self upon awakening constitutes itself as a thinking, ie, speaking, subject in its language, it needs that other self to whom its discourse is addressed. Emile Benveniste explains this fundamental psycho-linguistic mechanism as follows:

> C'est dans et par le langage que l'homme se constitue comme *sujet*;
> parce que le langage seul fonde en réalité, dans *sa* réalité qui est
> celle de l'être, le concept d'"ego."[3]

And he explains the 'dédoublement' of the thinking-speaking self:

> le "monologue" procède bien de l'énonciation. Il doit être posé,
> malgré l'apparence, comme une variété du dialogue, structure

fondamentale. Le "monologue" est un dialogue intériorisé,
formulé en "langage intérieur," entre un moi locuteur et un moi
écouteur. Parfois le moi locuteur est seul à parler; le moi écouteur
reste néanmoins présent; sa présence est nécessaire et suffisante
pour rendre signifiante l'énonciation du moi locuteur.[4]

Long before the new linguistics, Valéry had observed this phenomenon, naming it 'bouchoreille,' and adding 'un livre n'est après tout
qu'un extrait du monologue de son auteur. L'homme ou l'âme se
parle' (o II, p 479).

The intensity and sense of immediacy of the dawn fragments, as
well as their *moi*'s heightened subjectivity, are expressed more
densely by the verbal present tense. Thus Benveniste links subjectivity
and temporality in the self and its language:

> Il est aisé de voir que le domaine de la subjectivité s'agrandit encore
> et doit s'annexer l'expression de la temporalité. ... toujours la ligne
> de partage est une référence au "présent." ... il n'y a pas d'autre
> critère ni d'autre expression pour indiquer le temps où l'on *est*, que
> de le prendre comme "le temps où l'on *parle*." C'est là le moment
> éternellement "présent."

And as each dawn rises uniquely, the language of each aubade creates
a new *hic et nunc*, for, as the linguist explains, 'ce présent est
réinventé chaque fois qu'un homme parle parce que c'est, à la
lettre, un moment neuf, non encore vécu.'[5]

Valéry's prose aubades do not constitue a chronologically progressive series, nor do they reflect an artistic evolution from early to
mature to late poems. We have seen that the very structure of the
sequence of mobile fragments prohibits such a linear order, as a 'late'
sequence may frequently contain an 'early' fragment as one of its constituent parts. Thus I have necessarily avoided forcing these texts into
a one-dimensional, chronological, scheme but, rather, have attempted
to point to their multidimensional co-existence, in their infinite varia-
tion and identity, within this poetic universe in which each aubade,
like each *aube*, represents both renewal and repetition. For Valéry,
whose creative life was closely bound to the early morning hours,
dawn was clearly the most vivid manifestation of the ancient philosophical paradox of unity in variety, the One and the Many.

I opened this discussion, however, with an early prose poem, 'Purs
Drames,' and noted another such traditional piece in the first of the
'Trois Réveils.' But even the derivative 'Purs Drames' was already

marked by the characteristic Valéryan manner, not merely in its theme, but also structurally, as it already contained the mobile fragment in germ. Despite the Mallarméan and Rimbaldian influences which nourished it, it nevertheless showed a radical departure from its origins. In combining the theme of dawn with that of artistic vision, 'Purs Drames,' in Valéry's characteristic manner, links the dawn poem to one of the vital branches of the *œuvre* of which it is a fragment. For here the Symbolist Garden and the Fable of Eden, tradition and myth, become an exercise in and an exemplum of renewed and purified vision, where the protagonist is 'un œil pur.' 'Purs Drames' thus reaches out to another early Valéry text, the *Introduction à la Méthode de Léonard de Vinci*, the poet's treatise on the phenomenology of artistic perception, first published three years after our poem, an essay which in later years gradually grew into one of the principal supports of his total ideological and poetic edifice.

In the chapter 'Fragments,' we examined several dawn prose poems not incorporated into sequences and from different periods of the poet's creative life. These introduced us to some of the dominant motifs of all the aubades, such as the emergence of a still impersonal self – 'on n'est pas encore la personne qu'on est' – at dawn, that self's freedom from those specific personal traits which will later fix and imprison it in a particular person and day. We have seen this motif grow into a major theme of these poems; it participates in Valéry's myth of the 'Moi pur,' predominant throughout his poetry. Another characteristic motif encountered here was the exultation-anguish tension and the theme of lucid sadness, or sad lucidity, which reflects the essential light-darkness polarity of the moment – 'le jour commence par une lumière plus obscure que toute nuit.' Finally, the prose poem 'Laure' introduced an important actor of the matutinal drama, the soul, *anima*, with which the morning-*moi* is united 'dans une sphère unique au monde' at the privileged golden moment of 'l'aurore.'

In the 'A B C' poems we encountered three fragments, each of which constitutes a self-contained whole, while their underlying unity makes up the integrity of the sequence's tripartite configuration. 'A,' in which the awakening mind finds its still sleeping body at dawn, was the spirit's aubade, its passionate love song to the form which gave it life. The conscious mind and male spirit, *animus*, here was an angel of light wooing the still unconscious body, his mysterious female 'other half.'[6] In 'B' mind and body, united, greeted the new day, not without a nostalgia, however, for the origin, for a return to the source and 'la douceur de n'être pas.'[7] And as in 'C' the newly-risen self took possession of the new world, it was a self composed of an inner tension of opposing forces, an 'enfant aux cheveux gris' whose soul 'se sent femme endormie, ange fait de lumière,' a self reflecting the hour surrounding it, that moment which is both night and day. As the matutinal *moi* finally stepped out into the world, it felt an adoration for all things emerging in and with the sunlight. Possessed and enchanted by 'une amour infinie' the renewed self wishes to pray at this golden hour – 'or-oraison.' We have found this spiritual tonality again and again in these morning poems, the spirit's heightened lucidity and, at the same time, its love: 'je me rappelle des matins si purs, si premiers, si nus au sortir de la nuit, si jeunes et si frais que c'était à en pleurer de désespoir et d'amour' (c II, p 1289).

The posthumous sequence 'Trois Réveils' juxtaposed an early prose poem with two late fragments. And while 'Nuit à la caserne' still showed the influence of *A Rebours* and of the Goncourts' 'écriture artiste,' which that book revealed to the young Valéry, the fragments from the end of his life again link the theme of 'réveil' to dominant ones of the *œuvre*. The centre piece, which deals with the *moi*'s reflection in its *écriture*, as well as that of the text within the text, led us to a discussion of the 'persona' of these fragments and of the *Cahiers* from which so many of them were drawn. And we noted that the *ego scriptor* is a self stylized by its medium, rendered object by the text which reflects it. This is one of the meanings of the Narcisse, a major myth in Valéry's poetic universe. Narcisse is reflected in the mirror like the self in its introspective glance, and like the writer in his text. And just as Narcisse is recreated in an image which he loves, 'on écrit pour se rendre plus beau ... on écrit pour se recréer.' The theme of the writer-reader interrelationship, that of the creation of the 'writer-persona' and of the 'reader-persona' is diffused not merely throughout the *Cahiers*, but the essays and poetry as well.

After an ascent to the arid nihilism of the Solitaire, our second fragment led us back into the general rhythm and 'automatisme' of all things living. And this double tension of the spirit's transcendence into pure essential nothingness on the one hand, of its immersion and engulfment in and by existence on the other, pervades the aubades and all of Valéry's poetry. No theme is more fundamental to him. When the poet in our fragment says: 'je me perçois allant et agissant en plein automatisme,' he is, of course, including the very language in which he exists as a self in this 'automatisme.' No one was more aware than Valéry of the threatened disintegration of the thinking, ie, speaking, subject, the ominous and anguishing possibility of the 'death of Man' after the 'death of God.'[8] 'Qui parle?' is a constant Valéryan *Leitmotif*.

The sequence's final fragment reintroduced the notion of the 'Moi pur,' the ideal 'Zéro mathématique' as a privileged state of mind, in which nothing can be predicated of the *moi* except limitless virtuality.

The three 'Matins' again demonstrated the creative mechanism of the 'mobile fragment.' The first of these morning fragments, a highly lyrical celebration of the moment's promise and virtuality culminating in the metaphor of the seed – 'en germe, éternellement en germe, le plus haut degré universel d'existence et d'action' – fixed the fleeting instant before day's divisions; the separation of mind and soul, the self and the world with which it is emerging, and that of the world's mortal forms. This first 'Matin' also again marked the *moi*'s hesitations on the threshold of the day, and the regrets of the universal self at having to become a personal one, a person – 'que ne puis-je retarder d'être moi, paresser dans l'état universel?' I noted that this nostalgia linked our text not merely to other aubades, but also, for example, to 'Agathe,' whose *moi*-persona aspires after the same purity and universality. Our poem ended in a hymn to the sun and its light as symbol of 'l'esprit' and its lucidity. The second 'Matin' joined the celebration of dawn and the sun with that of the sea, another major element of Valéry's world, thus emphasizing the interrelationship of the themes of light and of the beginning – ô commencement!' – in this poetry. The final 'Matin' accentuated the dialectic of darkness and light, night and day, being and nothingness, in the stylistic refinement of its sentences with their chiasmatic structure, a device encountered repeatedly in these prose poems. Thus *forme* and *fond* are interwoven in the text as the binary nature of the perceiving mind is reflected in its language, which objectifies the moment's antithetical tension. It was a poetic logos, however, which made of this discourse an invocation 'à ce qui va être,' culminating in the image of the Annunciation, the 'salutation de l'ange qui annonce qu'on est fécondé, gros d'un jour nouveau.'

'Reprise' deals with its own *écriture*, with the world of letters and words upon the page, and so from the page before us the poem reaches out beyond to all the others, those 'successive approximations' and variations on the theme of dawn. In celebrating the poet's work, of which the poet is both possessor and possessed, the aubade introduced the theme of the creative process, and I noted that the creation of a poem, the process, interested Valéry more than the product. According to his poetics, moreover, a poem is never 'finished,' and its successive 'reprises' toward perfection, as well as the ideal of 'une diversité de variantes ou de solutions du même sujet,' which the poet himself compared to musical variations on a theme, perfectly describe these very prose aubades. 'Reprise I' concluded on the 'moral' struggle in this process in which the writer in creating the poem re-creates himself. The second fragment of the sequence dealt with the creative mind and reintroduced Valéry's notion of the awakening mind as analogous to a physical system of potential energy, or to the familiar 'Zéro mathématique.' In our poem this notion was objecti-fied in the 'attente pure' of the *moi* about to be struck by Damocles' sword, the state of heightened expectancy of the mind about to be ignited by a stroke of lightning. The vision of this mental state and moment led us to a discussion of Valéry's notion of 'l'Implexe,' 'ce en quoi et par quoi nous sommes éventuels,' 'ce qui est impliqué dans la nature de l'homme ou de moi, et qui n'est pas actuel,' a major theme of the *œuvre*. Thus this fragment, too, reached out to the poetic whole of which it is a part, to other texts, such as 'Agathe,' whose protago-nist arrives at this same state: the pure expectancy of an idea as yet unknown, that 'Idée maîtresse' born of pure chance, 'un effet sans cause, un accident qui est ma substance.' And in our morning poem again, this state belonged not merely to the mind, but to both intellect and affect, the 'esprit pur' and its 'âme,' a total self, ready for the igniting spark and for the day: 'je suis amour et soif et point de nom.'

'Notes d'aurore' celebrated language and the interdependence of language and perception in experience – 'voici la plus récente édition du vieux texte du Jour.' Again, an impassive world became animated and the morning meditation a prayer, and we recognized this dawn's ritual offerings from other aubades; the burning tree-tops, the roof-tiles glowing in the sun, and the morning mists among the leaves. Again, also, the soul in a mood of tenderness and sadness hesitated on the threshold of this new world and day, before giving in to life. Thus the familiar parallel of the *aube*'s and its *âme*'s precarious beginnings again revealed the fleeting moment's fragility: 'ce réel est encore en équi-libre avec le rien de tous ses songes.' And this precarious equilibrium of being and nothingness, this moment of becoming, was in the following sequence, 'Moments,' imaged by the scale with its two pans in balance.

'Moments' with its six fragments, all from different periods of the poet's creative life and each of a truly instantaneous nature, is a cha-racteristic dawn sequence, though three of the fragments are named after cities, reminding us of Valéry's substantial group of prose po-ems celebrating cities he loved. 'Nice' introduced the image of the balance – 'l'homme *pèse* ce qu'il *voit* et en est *pesé*' – thus figuring the dynamic state of equilibrium of opposing forces which distinguishes the aubades. Our poem's *moi*, moreover, was a poet-persona whose musings – 'je pense au poème de l'Intellect' – called to mind the very numerous references to a 'poem of the Intellect,' scattered throughout the *œuvre*. In discussing Valéry's notions of this ideal poem, we recognized that the finest realization of its concepts were in these very aubades themselves, one of their central themes being 'la sensibilité de l'intellect.'

The second fragment fixed a moment which somehow implied both being and nothingness, for it was pure becoming ('Aube – ce n'est pas l'aube') a moment both initial and final, while the third piece was again the sketch of a city: Grasse awakening at dawn under a miraculous light snow left by the night. The fourth fragment recreated the lovely image and movement of the swallow's sweeping flight, 'une belle hirondelle bleue et or' visiting the poet's room and thus interchanging darkness and light, inside and outside, and pivoting on the moment's dichotomy.

The last two fragments established the pastoral mood appropriate for the poet-persona's reflections on Vergil's bucolic mode, thus tying the ending of the sequence to its beginning with a poet's meditation on poetry: 'Un regard que je voudrais bien définir.'

The first of the four 'Petits Poèmes abstraits,' one of Valéry's most accomplished morning sequences, captured a pre-dawn, for 'Avant toute Chose' evoked the moment before the reappearance of both outer and inner worlds. Again, the one reflected the other: while the outer universe was still contained in its pre-Edenic futurity, the mind was in a state 'qui précède toutes les pensées particulières,' and 'l'âme jouit de sa lumière sans objets.' The rich virtuality and charged imminence of the universal *moi* and its *monde* at their privileged moment again recalled the universal hero, Léonard, of the 'Note et digression,' and the ideal of '*l'homme de l'esprit* [qui] doit se réduire sciemment à un refus d'être quoi que ce soit.' Our poem's *Stimmung* of mystic detachment from the world called for 'les mots les plus mystérieux et les plus téméraires,' the language and *Stimme* of prayer familiar from other morning poems. We found in the fragment, in fact, some of the very images and phrases from other aubades, for, as in prayer, these become formulaic in a ritual observance celebrated daily by a poet who asserted 'j'étais fait pour chanter Matines.'

'L'Unique' stressed the paradox of the uniqueness of each one of these uncountable dawns, the miracle of the first time for a thousandth time, which is also that of art and love. This paradox links the text to many others in the *œuvre*:

Tout va donc accomplir son acte solennel
De toujours reparaître incomparable et chaste,
Et de restituer la tombe enthousiaste
Au gracieux état du rire universel ('La Jeune Parque,' o i, p 106).

The innocent and renewed vision of an old world is one of the major themes of the *Introduction à la Méthode*, as well as of some of the Dialogues and lyric poetry. It is the very secret of poetry itself, for the poem, like each dawn, rises, phoenix-like, again and again from its own ashes. In celebrating renewal, 'L'Unique' pointed to one of the mind's basic, miraculous, saving laws: forgetfulness. The *moi* must obliterate its past so that anticipation and expectation may be new and unique each time. And we found this state of anticipation, when a virginal, refreshed morning-mind waits like a bride for its Master Notion, celebrated repeatedly not merely in Valéry's prose poetry, but in much of the lyric poetry as well. In the mysterious language announced in the preceding fragment, our poem then suggested the descent (into forgetfulness and non-being) and return of the self, its diurnal death and resurrection. The poem's images, moreover, recalled Sémiramis, 'reine-roi,' builder of cities and temples, born into, rising toward, and finally dying in the Sun's embrace. For Sémiramis is one of Valéry's symbols for the spirit's aspiration to transcend Time, while paradoxically utterly dependent on it.[9] Our fragment's chiasmatic sentences again stressed this pervading tension.

The tension of transcendence and imprisonment, of a self both in the world and beholding itself from the 'outside,' as it were, was the theme of 'Accueil du jour.' Here the *moi-double* was both actor and spectator as it stepped into the new day: 'j'entre en scène dans mon regard.' The tension of the whole fragment was that of 'être' and 'connaître,' of the *moi*'s anxious fear of being engulfed in the world's existence on the one hand, and of its temptation to transcendence into pure no-thingness on the other. Thus the poem objectified the Valéryan theme of the opposition of 'esprit' and 'vie' in suggesting the anguish and aspirations of the transcending mind, while at the same time painting and passionately celebrating the beauty of the mortal world: 'sur un toit rose et blond dorment quatre colombes; je songe vaguement à la sensation de leur chair dans la plume douce et chaude posée sur l'argile tiède, ô Vie...'

The closing fragment of the sequence, 'La Rentrée,' one of Valéry's rare prose poems about nightfall, introduced a feminine presence. And we noted that, while dawn's elevation is always unique and that of an unequaled, solitary *moi*, the oncoming night's weariness was shared: our persona addressed his evening reflections to the beloved, and the hour's terrors were projected into her – 'la fin du jour est femme.' Yet the fundamental oneness of the 'male' and of the 'female' within the self, one of the themes of the 'A B C' sequence, of 'Laure,' and of other aubades, was symbolized in our fragment's ending by the protective embrace shielding both lover and beloved from the threats of darkness and death.

In the first fragment of 'Méditation avant pensée,' we recognized the opening, 'Avant toute Chose,' of 'Petits Poèmes abstraits.' This mobile fragment became the longest of the new sequence. The second fragment deplored the mind's promiscuity, its inconstancies, and its impurity: 'toujours, tu préfères le hasard au vide, et le chaos au rien,' a complaint familiar from the *Cahiers* and sometimes even voiced in poems, such as the prose poem 'L'Amateur de poèmes.' The mind in its fickleness will run off with any notion met by chance, become the slave of its current 'Idée maîtresse'! This complaint against the haphazard activity of the mind is the natural obverse of Valéry's repeated celebration of the self's poised virtuality at dawn, before the day's demands have forced the *moi* into the finality of a chosen identity, and chosen actions. Our third Meditation lamented the mind's *gourmandise*, at once destructive and constructive, its 'instinct de dévorer ... de digérer définitivement les choses.' For the 'esprit,' like the organism, feeds on the world, transforming its raw material into its own substance.[10] In thus associating the mental with the libidinal, 'l'esprit' with hunger and sex, our text pointed again to the fundamental interdependence of *corps, esprit,* and *monde:* C E M. And, again, the *moi* was torn between refusal and acceptance, fasting and feasting, aspiring after an ideal transcendence of the world on which it must, however, feed to live.

The brief 'Considération matinale,' another mobile fragment, again presented the 'moi universel,' a self before the day's divisions. But the self was here seen from the outside, as an object, and not animated from within by a first-person voice. Thus the 'Considération' lacked the intensity of other aubades; its *moi*, moreover, remained outside the awakening world, 'en dehors du monde,' just as that world remained outside the fragment.

'A Grasse,' which I have chosen as the culminating sequence of the prose aubades, is on the contrary a hymn to the world by a voice that is part of it. In this poem, *corps, esprit,* and *monde* are in a harmonious equilibrium. As the human self accepts the world, the world becomes humanized, and as Man accepts Nature's mortality, he leaves his immortal mark on nature. In celebrating human industry in the cultivator of the earth and linking agriculture to architecture and art, the poet integrates poetry with the general human endeavour and the individual self with generations of men. The matutinal *moi* here reaches out not to transcend, but to embrace life and all mankind, and the final fragment in *vers libre* is the poet's offering in the communal ritual observance celebrating a new dawn, sung in by morning bells and birds and the poem of reconciliation.

But as we conclude our reading of these aubades, we do so without a 'concluding' poem. For Valéry's morning prose poems do not form a determinate structure or a closed cycle, but reappear again and again, always renewed, in his poetic universe, like the sun itself through the numberless dawns of the mutable world, like the immortal spirit of man through numberless generations of mortal men. Our texts constitute but a fragment of a larger whole, composed in part of other morning pieces dispersed throughout Valéry's work, both that which is published and that which is still hidden.[11] Thus, like the *œuvre* of which they are a part, they remain 'open,' and we read these fragments in the light and in the shadow of texts yet to be read.

Notes

CHAPTER ONE: INTRODUCTION

1 Cf. Octave Nadal, *A Mesure haute* (Paris: Mercure de France 1964) 229-46, 'Poèmes en prose.'
2 Suzanne Bernard, *Le Poème en prose de Baudelaire jusqu'à nos jours* (Paris: Librairie Nizet 1959).
   Mme Agathe Rouart-Valéry has just published an edition of a collection of Valéry's prose poems, *Alphabet* (Paris: Blaizot 1976); and she is presently preparing an édition of *Poésie brute*. These books will no doubt stimulate interest in Valéry's prose poetry.
3 Paul Valéry, *Cahiers*, ii, ed. Judith Robinson (Paris: Gallimard 1974; i, 1973) 1261. All quotations from Valéry's *Cahiers* will be from this edition, unless otherwise indicated, and noted by page number.
4 Charles Baudelaire, *Petits Poèmes en prose* (Paris: Garnier 1962) 7.
5 Cf. my *An Anatomy of Poesis: The Prose Poems of Stéphane Mallarmé* (Chapel Hill: North Carolina Studies in the Romance Languages and Literatures 1976).
6 For a recent lucid discussion of the 'Illuminations' and their relation to Rimbaud's *œuvre*, cf. Robert Greer Cohn, *The Poetry of Rimbaud* (Princeton: Princeton University Press 1973) 243-397.
7 J.-K. Huysmans, *A Rebours* (Paris: Editions Pasquelle 1968) 244.
8 *Lettres à quelques-uns* (Paris: Gallimard 1952) 26.
9 *Paul Valéry Oeuvres*, ii, ed. Jean Hytier (Paris: Gallimard 1960; i, 1957) 1386-92. All quotations from Valéry's work will be from this edition, unless otherwise indicated, and noted by page number.
10 Cf. Germaine Brée, 'The Break-up of Traditional Genres: Bataille, Leiris, Michaud,' *Bucknell Review* xxi (Fall-Winter 1973). Also Julia Kristeva, *La Révolution du langage poétique* (Paris: Editions du Seuil 1974) 289ff.

11 Cf. Florence de Lussy, *La Genèse de 'la Jeune Parque' de Paul Valéry* (Paris: Minard 1975) for an excellent recent study of the gradual growth of 'La Jeune Parque' out of its constituent – sometimes 'mobile' – fragments.

12 One is reminded that Mallarmé used various fragments in a mobile way in *Divagations*, eg, the 'Je dis: une fleur!...' which appears in 'Crise de vers' as well as in the 'Avant-dire au *Traité du Verbe.*' We recall, moreover, that the unbound (separate) pages of Mallarmé's projected 'Livre' (which Valéry probably did not know), provided a mobility that could alter interpretation, and thus constitute a full exploitation of the 'mobile fragment' in modern literature.

CHAPTER TWO: PURS DRAMES

1   Paul Valéry, 'Purs Drames,' *Entretiens politiques et littéraires* IV 24 (mars 1892) 102-4; *André Gide-Paul Valéry Correspondance 1890-1942*, ed. Robert Mallet (Paris: Gallimard 1955) 147.

2   Octave Nadal, 'Purs Drames,' *Cahiers du Sud* (avril 1957) 368-70; Nadal, *A Mesure haute* 237.

3   *Gide-Valéry Correspondance* 150.

4   For an excellent brief treatment of the theme, cf. James R. Lawler, *The Language of French Symbolism* (Princeton: Princeton University Press 1969) 185-217, 'Valéry's "Pureté".'

5   *Gide-Valéry Correspondance* 68.

6   Rimbaud, *Oeuvres Complètes* (Paris: Gallimard 1963) 193, 195.

7   *Oeuvres Complètes de Stéphane Mallarmé* (Paris: Gallimard 1945) 67.

8   Rimbaud, *Oeuvres* 175.

9   *Ibid*. 194.

10 At the same time Gide was elaborating his Symbolist garden in his 'Traité du Narcisse (Théorie du Symbole),' dedicated to Valéry. 'Chaste Eden! Jardin des Idées!' André Gide, *Romans* (Paris: Gallimard 1958) 5.

11 In a letter to Mallarmé of April 1891, Valéry writes: 'La poésie m'apparaît comme une explication du Monde délicate et belle, contenue dans une musique singulière et continuelle.' *Lettres à quelques-uns* 46.

12 Cf. '"*Au commencement était la Fable*" ce qu'il faut entendre ainsi: On appelle *Fable* tout commencement: origines, cosmogonies, mythologies...' (O II p 796).

13 A possible source here is Poe's 'Poetic Principle,' *Complete Tales and Poems* (New York: Vintage Books 1975) 905-6: 'It has been my purpose to suggest that, while this Principle itself is, strictly and simply, the Human Aspiration for Supernal Beauty, the manifestation of the Principle is

always found in *an elevating excitement of the Soul* ... or of that Truth which is the satisfaction of the Reason.'

14 For a conceptual exposition of Valéry's notion of artistic vision, cf. *Introduction à la Méthode de Léonard de Vinci*, a veritable treatise on the phenomenology of (artistic) perception (o I, esp. pp 1165ff.).

15 The 'une nue' of 's'évapore au calice du ciel, une nue' constitutes a marvelous Mallarméan ambiguity.

16 'Las de l'amer repos...,' Mallarmé, *Oeuvre* 36.

17 This ending had caused Valéry much difficulty. He writes to Gide: 'La fin est absurde, impénétrable – m'a ennuyé beaucoup.' *Correspondance Gide-Valéry* 147.

18 Mallarmé, *Oeuvres* 51.

19 'Les Vieilles Ruelles' of 1889, 'Pages Inédites' of 1891 (o I, pp 1599-1602) and 'Une Chambre Conjecturale,' posthumously published in *Le Figaro Littéraire* (15 octobre 1971). Cf. my 'A Dialectical Triad of Three Early Prose Poems by Paul Valéry: "Les Vieilles Ruelles," "Pages Inédites" and "Purs Drames",' to appear in the *Kentucky Romance Quarterly*.

20 *Gide-Valéry Correspondance* 43.

21 *Ibid.* 44.

22 *Ibid.* 59.

23 *Ibid.* 63.

24 *Ibid.* 83.

25 For an excellent English translation of 'Purs Drames,' cf. Paul Valéry: *Poems in the Rough*, ed. Jackson Mathews, Bollingen Series XLV 2 (Princeton: Princeton University Press 1969) 213-15.

CHAPTER THREE: FRAGMENTS

1 For a detailed exposition on Valéry's views on language and thought, cf. Jürgen Schmidt-Radefeldt, *Paul Valéry linguiste dans les 'Cahiers'* (Paris: Klincksieck 1970) esp. 34-38 and 169-71.

2 James R. Lawler, *The Poet as Analyst* (Berkeley: University of California Press 1974) 180. In this chapter, pp 166-200, Professor Lawler gives a most sensitive close reading of 'A l'Aurore'; his chapter 'Je pense..., je sens...,' 201-29, includes an equally fine treatment of 'L'Oiseau cruel.'

3 Cf. 'Introduction biographique' (o I, p 41): '1918 ... juin: il quitte Paris pour suivre M. Lebey qui se réfugie à l'Isle-Manière, dans la Manche. ... 10 juillet ... il lui envoie [à Mme Paul Valéry] aussi ce poème ['Le Platane'], écrit "dans cette riche région où l'arbre pousse comme l'herbe ... où la puissance végétale est comme inépuisable..."'

4 Berne-Jeffroy, *Présence de Valéry* (Paris: Plon 1944), 'Propos me concernant,' 3-61. Also in o II, pp 1505-36.

5 *D'Ariane à Zoé: Alphabet galant et sentimental* (Paris: Librairie de France 1930).

'Laure' here appears between Colette's 'Divine' and Paul Morand's 'Marion,' *La Nouvelle Revue Française* xxxvi 8-9 (janvier 1931).

6 Edmée de la Rochefoucauld, Valéry's friend and commentator of the *Cahiers*, *En Lisant les Cahiers de Paul Valéry* iii (Paris: Editions Universitaires 1967) 73-74, quotes from *Cahier* xxiii – which dates from 1940, the 'defeat,' a time which Valéry spent at the Charmettes, in Dinard, working on his 'Faust iii' – as follows:

A la ville des Charmettes ... Valéry trouve un petit volume de Charlotte Brontë, *Jane Eyre*, évocateur de Cette: "J'ai lu cette histoire en 84 au plus tard – il y a 56 ans au moins, et je n'en avais gardé que le souvenir d'une chose *trop* triste – en relation avec la maison du quai de l'Esplanade, avec le petit salon ... – à côté était le "grand salon" et ce piano (de 1840) qu'elle [Valéry's mother] ne touchait jamais, qui avait été celui de sa soeur Laura de Grassi, morte en 1848 du choléra – très jeune – qui abhorrait le temps perdu, etc.

Another of Valéry's friends and commentators, Lucienne Julien Cain, in *Trois Essais sur Paul Valéry* (Paris: Gallimard 1958) 57-8, evokes the same incident and 'le grand salon, toujours fermé, [qui] contenait le piano à queue sur lequel avait joué sa tante, Laura de Grassi, morte à seize ans du choléra...'

7 Cf. my 'The White Night of "Agathe": A Fragment by Paul Valéry,' *Essays in French Literature* 12 (Nedlands: The University of Western Australia 1975) 37-58.

8 Laura's fading image, the perfume of her dresses, her hair, rising from a past long dead, recalls the Hérodiade of the 'Ouverture ancienne,' 'Une voix, du passé longue évocation,' and 'Le parfum des cheveux endormis.' *Oeuvres* 42, 43.

9 For a sensitive discussion of the theme of autumn in Valéry, cf. Christine M. Crow, *Paul Valéry: Consciousness of Nature* (Cambridge: Cambridge University Press 1972) 142-5.

10 'Laure' is translated into English in Paul Valéry: *Poems in the Rough* (Princeton: Princeton University Press 1969) 235-6.

CHAPTER FOUR: THE TRILOGY A B C

1 *Commerce*: Cahiers trimestriels 5 (automne 1925) 4-14. In 'Introduction biographique' (o i, p 48), we find under 1924: 'Il s'occupe de la prochaine publication de la revue *Commerce*, cahiers trimestriels qu'il dirige avec Valéry Larbaud, et Léon Paul Fargue. – Septembre: Il séjourne à

Deauville chez la princesse de Bassiano, fondatrice de cette revue.'
Commerce was somewhat short-lived, from 1924 to 1932.

For an English translation of the prose poems 'ABC,' and of many of the
prose aubades, cf. Paul Valéry, *Poems in the Rough* (Princeton: Princeton
University Press 1969) 223-8. In the Notes to 'ABC,' p 319, the editor in-
forms us as follows: 'In the 1920's Valéry was planning a collection of
prose poems to be titled *Alphabet*. The ABC poems were written for that
series, which was never completed. In the *Valéryanum* (a collection of
Valéry's published works made by Julien P. Monod, and now in the
Bibliothèque Jacques Doucet in Paris) there are several prose poems in
typescript probably written for *Alphabet*. They are *Attente* "Waiting";
Midi "Midday"; *Le Bain* "The Bath"; *Laure* "Laura"; *L'Unique* "The
Unique"; *Accueil du jour* "Greeting the Day"; and *La Rentrée* "The Return".' Some of these pieces do appear in the *Pléiade* edition; some have
been published by Valéry in other series, such as *'L'Unique,' 'Accueil du
jour,'* and *'La Rentrée'* under the heading *'Petits Poèmes abstraits'* in *La
Revue de France* in 1932. In both the 1956 and the 1971 Valéry exposi-
tions at the Bibliothèque Nationale, there was on display an autograph
Cahier of these poems, with the following note (1956 Catalogue #313):
'ABC' Cahier autographe: 'Suite de courts "poèmes en prose" com-
mençant chacun par une lettre différente, et disposés suivant l'ordre
alphabétique. Ils évoquent les diverses heures de la journée. Les trois
premiers ont paru séparément dans la revue *Commerce*, un autre parmi
les "Petits poèmes abstraits," publiés en 1932 par *la Revue de France*. En
1939 Paul Valéry avait songé à publier l'ensemble en une edition de
luxe, dont la maquette avait été entreprise. La guerre l'empêcha de
mener son projet à bien.'

2 Paul Valéry, *Morceaux choisis* (Paris: Gallimard 1930) 51-2.

3 The poem's opening sentence, with the change from 'sommeil' to
'soleil' – 'Au commencement sera le Soleil' – has become the title of the
free-verse rendition of a fragment of the poem in the 'Poèmes' section of
Histoires brisées (O II, pp 461-2).

4 Cf. Robert Greer Cohn, *Toward the Poems of Mallarmé* (Berkeley: University of California Press 1965) especially 269-70. Professor Cohn discusses
these 'ABC's of Poetry' in an article by that title, in *Comparative Literature* 2
(1962) 187-91.

5 Cf. Nicole Celeyrette-Pietri, 'Le Jeu du je,' in *Paul Valéry Contemporain*
(Paris: Klincksieck 1974) 11-25, for a discussion of the 'interior dialogue'
in Valéry, and in the 'ABC' poem(s). Mme Celeyrette-Pietri again discusses the first of these three poems in 'Au Commencement sera le sommeil: quelques réflexions sur un poème en prose' in *Cahiers Paul Valéry
I: Poétique et poésie* (Paris: Gallimard 1975) 205-24.

6 For a recent discussion of the 'insular self,' cf. Ludmilla M. Wills, *Le Regard contemplatif chez Valéry et Mallarmé* (Amsterdam: Rodopi NV 1974) 81-6.

7 Il n'est pour ravir un monde
   De blessure si profonde
   Qui ne soit au ravisseur
   Une féconde blessure,
   Et son propre sang l'assure
   D'être le vrai possesseur (o ɪ, p 113).

8 Marcel Raymond, *Paul Valéry et la tentation de l'esprit* (Neuchatel: A la Baconnière 1948) 55-9, in a brief discussion of the 'A B C' fragments, notes the shift from first to third person in the fragments 'A' and 'B.'

9 Cf. Lawler, *The Poet as Analyst*, 135-6 and 204-6, for a brief discussion of 'C.'
   'CEM le présent est la liaison de la sensation corporelle avec la perception des choses environnantes et avec celle de la production psychique. Il est donc perception d'un accord C E M des liaisons entre ces constituants' (c ɪ, p 1141).

10 'L'Unique,' 'Petits Poèmes abstraits,' *La Revue de France* (janvier 1915) 48-9.

11 Recall the frequent sketches in the *Cahiers* of the uroboros, the snake, or double snake, swallowing its tail.

12 Cf. Hugette Laurenti, *Paul Valéry et le théâtre* (Paris: Gallimard 1973) 112-17 for Valéry's admiration of the liturgy.

13 This dialectic of darkness and light is well seen by Jean Levaillant, 'Paul Valéry et la lumière,' *Association Internationale des Etudes françaises*, Cahiers 22 (May 1968) 187: 'Ainsi, la lumière qui donne le sens universel à ce qui est, n'existe pas sans la vie qu'elle est capable de faire connaître, mais qu'elle reste incapable de faire comprendre.'

14 J.-L. Faivre, *Paul Valéry et le thème de la lumière* (Paris: Lettres Modernes 1975). In the first chapter the author discusses several of Valéry's morning prose poems, as well as 'Aurore.'

CHAPTER FIVE: TROIS REVEILS

1 *Paul Valéry vivant* (Marseilles: Cahiers du Sud 1946) 273-6. For an English translation of 'Trois Réveils,' cf. the final volume of the *Collected Works of Paul Valéry* in the Bollingen Series (Princeton: Princeton University Press 1975), vol. xv, *Moi* 15-18.

2 Cf. o ɪ, p 17. In *Paul Valéry vivant*, between pp 56 and 57, is the reproduction of a photo of Valéry in the uniform of the 122nd Regiment, taken in 1889.

3 Huysmans, *A Rebours* 244.

4 Cf. my 'Mallarméan and Other Affinities in an Early Prose Poem by
   Paul Valéry: "Une Chambre conjecturale",' *The French Review*, 2 xi
   (1977).

5 How 'imprisoned' the young poet felt during the beginning of his 'service militaire' is evident from an undated letter to Albert Dugrin, *Lettres à
   quelques-uns* 11, which the editor designates as 'qui doit avoir été
   écrite à la fin de l'année 1889, peu après le début du service militaire,' and in which Valéry says: 'Voilà que j'ai déjà un mois
   d'escalvage, un mois de douloureux sacrifice à la Patrie! ... Pour moi, la
   Patrie n'est pas sous les plis d'un drapeau ni une terre limitée; ma patrie, ce sont mes idées, mes rêves, et ceux-là sont mes compatriotes qui
   les détiennent avec moi.'

6 Robinson, *Cahiers* i, p 223. Both parts of our second 'réveil' are together,
   spaced into three paragraphs, occupying pp 99 to 100 of the facsimile
   edition of Paul Valéry *Cahiers* xxviii (1943-4) (Paris Centre National de la
   Recherche Scientifique 1961).

7 Cf. Huguette Laurenti, *Paul Valéry et le théâtre* (Paris: Gallimard 1973)
   260: 'Le dédoublement qu'implique la connaissance fait que la "vie con-
   sciente" est théâtre.'

8 Cf. Roman Jakobson, *Questions de poétique* (Paris: Editions du Seuil 1973)
   120: 'Toute expression verbale stylise et transforme, en un certain sens,
   l'événement qu'elle décrit.' This whole chapter, 'Qu'est-ce que la
   poésie?', pp 113-26, in discussing the interrelationship of the poetry and
   the journal of the poet Mácha, deals with the fundamental problem of
   Dichtung und Wahrheit.

9 Cf. Robinson, *Cahiers* i, pp 222 and *passim*. The seventy-three-year-old
   Valéry had just undergone a serious illness.

10 *Ebauches de 'Mon Faust,'* in La Table Ronde 1 (Paris: Les Editions du
   Centre 1944).

11 In the original *Cahier* (cnrs, Vol. xxviii), this sentence is accentuated by
   three vertical marginal lines. And, curiously, the entry following our
   'réveil' is annotated 'Faust – Solitaire.'

CHAPTER SIX: THREE MATINS

1 *La Revue de France* 14 (15 décembre 1926) 762-6.

2 For an English translation of 'Matin,' cf. Paul Valéry: *Poems in the Rough*
   (Princeton: Princeton University Press 1969) 167-9.

3 We recall here that the 'a b c' prose aubades were published in the review
   Commerce (cf. note 1, Chapter 2), whose title has its source in Saint-John
   Perse's epic poem, 'Anabase,' *Oeuvres complètes* (Paris: Gallimard 1972)

93: '...j'arrêtais sur les marchés déserts ce pur commerce de mon âme, parmi vous.'

4 In 'Réponse première,' Valéry says: 'la première perception est, avant toute chose, celle de *lumière et de Voir*' (c II, p 199).

5 The structural refinement of both this and the opening sentence are subsequent to the 1913 *Cahier* fragment.

6 This moment and its verbalization recall a similar one from Rimbaud's 'Déserts de l'amour,' whose *moi* is 'ému jusqu'à la mort par le murmure du lait du matin...' *Oeuvres complètes* 171.

7 An English translation of this 'Matin' is to be found in *Poems in the Rough* 171.

8 Cf. Paul Valéry, *Cahiers* VIII (Paris: Centre National de la Recherche Scientifique 1961), 259.

9 We should here like to draw attention to a discussion by Jacques Derrida of the 'sources' of Valéry, even those 'écartées.' In 'Qual Quelle: les sources de Valéry,' in *Marges de la philosophie* (Paris: Editions de Minuit 1972) 325-63, the author takes as point of departure Valéry's prose poem 'Louanges de l'eau,' written in 1935 for la Source Perrier; and he points to certain *hantises de l'origine* in Valéry which are manifest, it appears, under the sign of water.

10 For an English translation of this 'Matin,' cf. *Poems in the Rough* 66-8.

11 It is for this reason that Valéry subjected language to the most critical considerations, which lie beyond the limits of this study. He reminds us: 'Il faut bien penser à ceci: le langage a presque tout fait, et entre autres choses il a fait l'esprit' (c I, p 405).

CHAPTER SEVEN: REPRISE

1 For an English translation of 'Reprise,' cf. Paul Valéry: *Poems in the Rough* (Princeton: Princeton University Press 1969) 171-3.

2 The allusion to Acts 17: 28 – 'car en lui nous avons la vie, le mouvement, et l'être. C'est ce qu'ont dit aussi quelques-uns de vos poètes: Nous sommes de sa race...' – is obvious and ironic.

3 Jacques Derrida, *De la Grammatologie* (Paris: Editions de Minuit 1967) 95: '*La trace est en effet l'origine absolue du sens en général. Ce qui revient à dire, encore une fois, qu'il n'y a pas d'origine absolue du sens en général. La trace est la différence qui ouvre l'apparaître et la signification.*'

4 This prose poem was printed posthumously by J.-P. Monod in the form of a 'nain' (in 64) in twelve *exemplaires*, one of which is in the Bibliothèque Nationale (Special Collections). There it bears the title: 'Paul Valéry Invocation.' It was further published in 1953 in *Ars Specta-*

cles under the title 'Un Poème inédit de Paul Valéry.' Its rhythm
recalls the 'versets Claudeliens.'

5 The lectures given by Valéry, who was appointed to the Chair for Poetry
   at the Collège de France in 1937, were reproduced in *Yggdrasil*, no's. 9
   (décembre 1937), to 34 (25 février 1939). Our quotation is from the
   lecture given on 17 December 1937, no. 9, p 144.
6 S. Yeschua, '"Substitutions" et poétique chez Valéry' in *Cahiers Paul
   Valéry. I: Poétique et poésie* (Paris: Gallimard 1975) 145-6.
7 *Yggdrasil*, no. 9, pp 141-2.
8 Two versions of this piece were published posthumously in *La Nouvelle
   Revue Française* (août 1971) 12-16, with several 'Alphabet' prose poems.
9 This expectation of and readiness for the decisive event recalls 'Abeille'
   (o I, p 118).

CHAPTER EIGHT: NOTES D'AURORE

1 Cf. Paul Valéry, *Analects* (Princeton: Princeton University Press 1970)
   462-4, for an English translation of 'Notes d'aurore.'
2 Cf. 'La Jeune Parque's' magnificent aube: 'Feu vers qui se soulève une
   vierge de sang/Sous les espèces d'or d'un sein reconnaissant!' (o I,
   p 110).

CHAPTER NINE: MOMENTS

1 In the Bollingen Series, the translation of 'Moments' appears in *Poems in
   the Rough* (Princeton: Princeton University Press 1969) 37-9.
2 Valéry visited Nice frequently, especially from 1933 on, when he became 'administrateur du Centre méditerranéen' there (o I, p 59). The
   poet fulfilled this function until 1941, when the Vichy government
   divested him of it.
3 Maurice Toesca, 'Paul Valéry: *Agathe*,' *Nouvelle Revue Française*
   (mai 1957) 911.
4 Cf. Marcel Raymond, *Paul Valéry et la tentation de l'esprit* (Neuchatel: A la
   Baconnière 1948).
5 Rimbaud, who wanted to radically reshape language into his instrument,
   understood, as did Mallarmé and Valéry, that the poet, at the same
   time, might well be the instrument of the language which speaks through
   him: 'Je pense: on devrait dire on me pense ... Je est un autre. Tant pis
   pour le bois qui se trouve violon' (*Oeuvres* 249).
6 A possible source for 'le Zaïmph' and its associations might be
   Flaubert's *Salammbô*.

7 Our 'Moment' of surprise and delight at the snow in the morning sun recalls 'Neige':

Quel silence, battu d'un simple bruit de bêche!...

Je m'éveille, attendu par cette neige fraîche
Qui me saisit au creux de ma chère chaleur.
...
Oh! combien de flocons, pendant ma douce absence,
Durent les sombres cieux perdre toute la nuit!
...(o i, pp 325-6).

8 Cf. Christine M. Crow, *Paul Valéry: Consciousness of Nature* (Cambridge: Cambridge University Press 1972), especially 'Living Things' 104-6, for the presence of birds in Valéry's poetry.

CHAPTER TEN: PETITS POEMES ABSTRAITS

1 Paul Valéry, 'Petits Poèmes abstraits,' *La Revue de France* (janvier 1932) 47-52.

2 For English translations of the poems, cf. *Poems in the Rough* (Princeton: Princeton University Press 1969) 61-2 for 'Avant toute Chose,' pp 237-42 for the other three pieces.

3 That Valéry himself conceived it so is evident from the following *Cahier* entry about these poems: 'A l'Académie Bazin me tire à part et à mon immense étonnement me fait de grands compliments sur mes *Poèmes Abstraits* de la *Revue de France*! Le ton mystique de ces pièces – a dû l'impressionner. Je tombe des nues. L'obscurité de ces essais dont je suis fort peu satisfait ne l'a pas rebuté ni choqué!...' (c i, p 271).

4 'Agnostic' must be used with caution concerning Valéry. In a 1936 *Cahier* entry, he says: 'On m'a dit *agnostique* – Mais on l'entend: celui qui croit que tel problème est insoluble – tandisque je dis bien plus souvent: celui qui croit que le problème n'a point de vérification' (c ii, p 667). I mean 'agnostic' as here applied to Valéry in the sense of his attitude being 'noncommittal.'

5 Valéry likened the mind's cyclical movement ('je ne sais comment bâtir ces définitions de fonction, phase, cycle qui permettraient de suivre les variations multiformes de l'homme. Cependant je *sens* ces notions' [c i, p 893]) to the transformation of a substance from one state to another in the cycle of a closed thermodynamic system; indeed, the laws of thermodynamics became his favourite instrument of psychological analysis. Cf. Judith Robinson, *Analyse de l'esprit dans les Cahiers de Valéry* (Paris: José Corti 1963) esp. 64ff.

6 'Propos sur la poésie' (o I, pp 1371-8). In this crucial text, Valéry also defines the key notion of the 'univers poétique,' and elaborates the classical comparison of poetry to dance. He makes here, moreover, his most explicit statement about the functions of 'forme' and 'fond' in poetry.

7 This psychological experience appears almost universal in the exceptional creative individual, from the 'Night of Pascal' and Descartes' similar crisis to Mallarmé's 'Crise de Tournon,' and finally Valéry's own 'Nuit de Gênes' of 1892, which resulted literally in a death of poetry before it could be reborn after some twenty years of ascetic abstention and absence, 'la période aigüe.'

8 Paul Valéry, *Cahiers* (Paris: Centre National de la Recherche Scientifique 1961) Vols. XIV, p 574, XXVI, p 291. Ned Bastet discusses the opposition of 'l'esprit' to the cyclical operation of nature, of which it partakes, in 'Faust et le cycle' in *Entretiens sur Paul Valéry* (La Haye et Paris: Mouton 1968) 115-28.

9 The 'bel *Aujourd'hui* que tu es – *Aujourd'hui* qui m'entoures' recalls Mallarmé's 'Le vierge, le vivace et le bel aujourd'hui,' *Oeuvres* 67.

10 One of the most accomplished of these is 'Sur la Jetée de Cannes,' which Valéry wrote in 1936 for *Le Rotary* (no. 87, mars, 9-10). In this piece he evokes all the refulgence of the sunset over the harbour, before its final decomposition.

11 The vocabulary here is strongly reminiscent of Baudelaire's 'Correspondances': 'Comme de longs échos qui de loin se confondent/Dans une ténébreuse et profonde unité,/Vaste comme la nuit et comme la clarté,' *Les Fleurs du mal* (Paris: Garnier 1961) 13.

12 This 'jour décapité' recalls Mallarmé's 'Cantique de Saint Jean,' 'Le soleil que sa halte/Surnaturelle exalte/Aussitôt redescend/Incandescent,' *Oeuvres* 49, and above all Apollinaire's final line of 'Zone,' 'Soleil cou coupé.' *Alcools* (Paris: Larousse 1972) 43.

13 The femininity of the sunset – contrasting with the virile sunrise – is most beautifully versified in one of Valéry's own favourite passages of the 'Fragments du Narcisse':

  O douceur de survivre à la force du jour,
  Quand elle se retire enfin rose d'amour,
  Encore un peu brûlante, et lasse, mais comblée,
  Et de tant de trésors tendrement accablée
  Par de tels souvenirs qu'ils empourprent sa mort,
  Et qu'ils la font heureuse agenouiller dans l'or,
  Puis s'étendre, se fondre, et perdre sa vendange,
  Et s'éteindre en un songe en qui le soir se change (o I, p 123).

CHAPTER ELEVEN: MEDITATION AVANT PENSEE

1 For an English translation of 'Méditation avant pensée,' cf. *Poems in the Rough* (Princeton: Princeton University Press 1969) 61-3.
2 Diderot, *Oeuvres romanesques* (Paris: Garnier 1962) 395.
3 The narrator of Gide's *Nourritures terrestres* – which also celebrate their author's friendship with Valéry-Ambroise ('à Montpellier, le jardin botanique. Je me souviens...') – also prefers the moment of his hunger over that of its satisfaction: 'Ce que j'ai connu de plus beau sur la terre,/Ah! Nathanaël! c'est ma faim.' *Romans* 167.

CHAPTER TWELVE: LA CONSIDERATION MATINALE

1 For English translations of these two versions, cf. *Analects* (Princeton: Princeton University Press 1970) 400, 486-7.
2 *Cahiers du Sud* (juin 1938) 409-11. Only two pieces of this sequence of nine fragments, the one discussed here and the free-verse 'Petit Psaume du matin,' are actually aubades. The other pieces are about dreams, the functioning of the mind in general, and, in two cases, about literature.

CHAPTER THIRTEEN: A GRASSE

1 For an English translation of 'A Grasse,' cf. *Poems in the Rough* (Princeton: Princeton University Press 1969) 21-3. The fact that our third fragment was incorporated in the sequence 'Fruits de mer,' which Valéry published in 1940 in the luxurious art magazine *Verve* (No. 8, Vol. II), pp 22-5, points again not merely to the 'mobile fragment,' but also to the close interrelationship of the themes of dawn and of the sea in this poetic universe.
2 The question of Valéry's use of anagrams has recently been raised by Professors Moutote, Schmidt-Radefeldt, Mignot, Celeyrette-Pietri, Laurenti, and Robinson in their discussion at the occasion of the Séminaire Trimestriel du Centre d'Etudes Valéryennes on the theme of 'Valéry et la science du langage.' Cf. *Bulletin des Etudes Valéryennes*, Montpellier, Université Paul Valéry, No. 8 (janvier 1976) 38.
3 Thus the sensitive rendition of the Bollingen Series translation *Poems in the Rough* (Princeton: Princeton University Press 1969) 21.
4 'L'homme qui pioche' may be an allusion on Valéry's part to the emblem of the original Lemerre edition of Leconte de Lisle. The poet, in this emblem, is graphically likened to a labourer.
5 We recall that Valéry published the third fragment of the prose poem sequence 'ABC' subsequently separately in *vers libre*.

6 A *Cahier* entry from 1924 demonstrates the rigorous specifications of a
   'commande': '80 pages x 32 lignes x 50 lettres. J'ai à faire (pour mettre
   des paroles autour des gravures de Beltrand) un texte ... les gravures
   comprennent 3 et 1 et 4 planches – 4 moindres, 3 plus grandes, 1 impor-
   tante. Il y a 40 grandes pages à fournir ... Je vais essayer de remplir cette
   tâche qui doit être assez bien payée et dont je ne vois pas du tout le
   contenu, par approximations successives à partir des conditions quanti-
   tatives' (c II, p 1014). And in the same entry, Valéry continues: 'Cette
   marche paradoxale est au fond la marche vraie – celle qui serait générale en littérature sans les idées fausses, vagues et préconçues sans
   examen qui règnent en ce royaune de l'absurde. Car c'est lier durée,
   fond, et forme de la construction. ... Cette création artificielle est au fond
   la *naturelle*.' Again, this text links poetic production as a solving of tech-
   nical problems imposed by the consumer, to human industry in a general
   sense. I should again like to recall Valéry's collaboration with Valery
   Larbaud on the revue *Commerce,* and the origin of that review's name in
   the lines of Saint-John Perse's 'Anabase,' (quoted above note 3, Chapter
   5), which points to the 'literary commerce' that existed between Valéry
   and his great contemporary poets.
7 Laurette, Pierre, *Le Thème de l'arbre chez Valéry* (Paris: Librairie Klincksieck 1967). Cf. also the less well-known prose poem 'Arbre' (o II, p 659).

CHAPTER FOURTEEN: CONCLUSION

1 Jean Thibaudeau, 'Le Roman comme autobiographie' in *Tel Quel: Théorie
   d'ensemble* (Paris: Editions du Seuil 1968) 215-16. It is interesting to
   note that Valéry, one of the severest critics of the traditional novel,
   should in his predilection for and his practice of the fragment and of the
   sequence already presage, in a sense, one of the forms the new and
   non-traditional *roman* was to take. The most recent study on Valéry
   and the novel is Silvio Yeschua's *Valéry, le roman et l'œuvre à faire*
   (Paris: Minard 1976).
2 Valéry's notions on the indissolubility of *forme* and *fond* are most poetically imaged in the famous 'pendule qui oscille entre deux points
   symétriques. Supposez que l'une de ces positions extrêmes représente
   la forme ... Associez, d'autre part, à l'autre point ... toutes les valeurs
   significatives' (o I, p 1332). In the same text, 'Poésie et pensée abstraite,'
   he continues, 'entre la Voix et la Pensée, entre la Pensée et la Voix,
   entre la Présence et l'Absence, oscille le pendule poétique. Il résulte de
   cet analyse que la valeur d'un poème réside dans l'indissolubilité du
   son et du sens' (p 1333). One recalls that Roman Jakobson profitably
   adopted this Valéryan image.

3 Emile Benveniste, *Problèmes de linguistique générale* (Paris: Gallimard 1966, ii: 1974) i 259.

4 *Ibid.* ii 85-6.

5 *Ibid.* 74.

6 Cf. C.G. Jung, *Psyche and Symbol* (New York: Anchor Books 1958) 142: 'it is readily understandable that the primordial image of the hermaphrodite should reappear in modern psychology in the guise of the male-female antithesis, in other words as *male* consciousness and personified *female* unconsciousness.' Cf. also Erich Neumann, *The Origins and History of Consciousness* (Princeton: Princeton University Press 1954) 42: 'But one thing, paradoxical though it may seem, can be established at once as a basic law: even in woman, consciousness has a masculine character. The correlation "consciousness-light-day" and "unconsciousness-darkness-night" holds true regardless of sex. Consciousness, as such, is masculine even in women, just as the unconscious is feminine in men.'

7 *Ibid.* 18, 'in every individual life, consciousness reexperiences its emergence from the unconscious in the growth of childhood, and every night in sleep, dying with the sun, it sinks back into the depths of the unconscious, to be born in the morning and to begin the day anew.'

8 For a most recent discussion of the rejection of the notion of the 'subject' in Structuralist thought, cf. Jonathan Culler, *Structuralist Poetics* (Ithaca: Cornell University Press 1975) esp. 26ff. Cf. also Jean-Marie Benoist, *La Révolution structurale* (Paris: Grasset 1975) esp. 55ff. and *passim*.

9 Sémiramis literally 'ascends' to her fatal marriage with the sun, while the Spirit's involvement in Time is frequently figured as a 'descent.' Cf. this fragment from *Mélange*: 'Un esprit allait voir cesser son état; il devait tomber dans le Temps; s'incarner: "Tu vas *vivre*!" C'était *mourir* pour lui; Quel effroi! Descendre dans le Temps' (o i, p 299)!

10 Cf. Neumann, *The Origin* 317-18: 'In this sense all knowledge rests on an aggressive act of incorporation. The psychic system, and to an even greater extent consciousness itself, is an organ for breaking up, digesting, and then rebuilding the objects of the world and the unconscious, in exactly the same way as our bodily digestive system decomposes matter physiochemically and uses it for the creation of new structures.'

11 A beautiful new prose aubade which has come to light (from the *inédits*) since my work on this book began is that of the awakening Lust, 'Eveil de Lust et Monologue,' just published with 'Textes inédits, Quatrième acte de "Lust",' by Ned Bastet in the *Cahiers Paul Valéry 2: 'Mes Théâtres'* (Paris: Gallimard 1977) 55-6: 'Bonjour, jour ... Fils de jour, père de jours ... O tout jeune mais encore semblable à tous les autres et déjà différent de tout autre. O jour vierge comme je suis vierge. Il me semble que je suis encore sans nom, sans âge, sans désirs, sans regrets, comme

une lumière qui n'est que lumière qui ne sait rien encore sans choses,
bien séparée de ce qu'elle va leur faire dire en les touchant. Ainsi,
moi ... Je me sens toute amour, rien qu'amour, mais absolue amour. Et il
n'y a rien encore que cette tendre amour illumine...'

Bibliography

WORKS CITED

Valéry, Paul *Oeuvres*, I & II (Paris: Gallimard 1957 & 1960)
- *Cahiers*, I & II (Paris: Gallimard 1973 & 1974)
- *Cahiers*, 28 Vols (Paris: Centre National de la Recherche Scientifique 1961)
- *Alphabet* (Paris: Blaizot 1976)
- *Morceaux choisis* (Paris: Gallimard 1930)
Paul Valéry vivant (Marseilles: *Cahiers du Sud* 1946)
Valéry, Paul *Cours de Poétique* nos. 9-34 (Paris: *Yggdrasil*, décembre 1937 to février 1939)
- 'ABC,' *Commerce*: Cahiers trimestriels (automne 1925)
- 'Ebauche de "Mon Faust",' *La Table ronde*, no. 1 (Les Editions du centre 1944)
- 'Laure,' *La Nouvelle Revue Française* XXXVI (janvier 1931)
- 'Petits Poèmes abstraits,' *La Revue de France* (janvier 1932)
- 'Purs Drames,' *Entretiens politiques et littéraires* IV (mars 1892)
- 'Rêves,' *La Revue de France* (décembre 1926)
- 'Une Chambre conjecturale,' *Le Figaro littéraire* (octobre 1971)
Paul Valéry, Analects, Bollingen Series XLV (Princeton: Princeton University Press 1970)
Paul Valéry, Poems in the Rough, Bollingen Series XLV (Princeton: Princeton University Press 1969)
Paul Valéry, Moi, Bollingen Series XLV (Princeton: Princeton University Press 1975)

André Gide-Paul Valéry Correspondance 1890-1942 (Paris: Gallimard 1955)
Lettres à quelques-uns (Paris: Gallimard 1952)
Paul Valéry, Exposition du centenaire (Paris: Bibliothèque Nationale 1971)
Paul Valéry (Paris: Bibliothèque Nationale 1956)

Apollinaire, Guillaume *Alcools* (Paris: Larousse 1972)
Baudelaire, Charles *Les Fleurs du mal* (Paris: Garnier 1961)
– *Petits Poèmes en prose* (Paris: Garnier 1962)
Diderot *Oeuvres romanesques* (Paris: Garnier 1962)
Gide, André *Romans* (Paris: Gallimard 1958)
Huysmans, J.-K. *A Rebours* (Paris: Editions Pasquelles 1968)
Mallarmé, Stéphane *Oeuvres complètes* (Paris: Gallimard 1945)
Perse, Saint-John *Oeuvres complètes* (Paris: Gallimard 1972)
Poe, Edgar Allan *The Complete Tales and Poems* (New York: Vintage Books 1975)
Rimbaud, *Oeuvres complètes* (Paris: Gallimard 1963)

Benoist, Jean-Marie *La Révolution structurale* (Paris: Grasset 1975)
Benveniste, Emile *Problèmes de linguistique générale* I & II (Paris: Gallimard 1966 & 1974)
Bernard, Suzanne *Le Poème en prose de Baudelaire jusqu'à nos jours* (Paris: Nizet 1959)
Berne-Jeffroy *Présence de Valéry* (Paris: Plon 1944)
Bulletin des Etudes Valéryennes, Montpellier, Université Paul Valéry, no. 2 (janvier 1976)
Cohn, Robert Greer *Toward the Poems of Mallarmé* (Berkeley: University of California Press 1965)
– *The Poetry of Rimbaud* (Princeton: Princeton University Press 1973)
Crow, Christine M. *Paul Valéry: Consciousness of Nature* (Cambridge: Cambridge University Press 1972)
Culler, Jonathan *Structuralist Poetics* (Ithaca: Cornell University Press 1975)
Derrida, Jacques *De la Grammatologie* (Paris: Editions de Minuit 1967)
– *Marges de la philosophie* (Paris: Editions de Minuit 1972)
Faivre, J.-L. *Paul Valéry et le thème de la lumière* (Paris: Lettres Modernes 1975)
Franklin, Ursula *An Anatomy of Poesis: The Prose Poems of Stéphane Mallarmé* (Chapel Hill: North Carolina Studies in the Romance Languages and Literatures 1976)
Jakobson, Roman *Questions de poétique* (Paris: Editions du Seuil 1973)
Julien-Cain, Lucienne *Trois Essais sur Paul Valéry* (Paris: Gallimard 1958)
Jung, C.G. *Psyche and Symbol* (New York: Anchor Books 1958)
Kristeva, Julia *La Révolution du langage poétique* (Paris: Editions du Seuil 1974)
Laurenti, Huguette *Paul Valéry et le théâtre* (Paris: Gallimard 1973)
Lawler, James R. *The Language of French Symbolism* (Princeton: Princeton University Press 1969)
– *The Poet as Analyst* (Berkeley: University of California Press 1974)
Laurette, Pierre *Le Thème de l'arbre chez Valéry* (Paris: Klincksieck 1967)

Lussy, Florence de *La Genèse de 'La Jeune Parque' de Paul Valéry*
   (Paris: Minard 1975)

Nadal, Octave *A Mesure haute* (Paris: Mercure de France 1964)

Neumann, Erich *The Origins and History of Consciousness* (Princeton:
   Princeton University Press 1954)

Raymond, Marcel *Paul Valéry et la tentation de l'esprit* (Neuchatel: A la
   Baconniere 1948)

Robinson, Judith *Analyse de l'esprit dans les Cahiers de Valéry* (Paris: Corti
   1963)

la Rochefoucauld, Edmée de *En lisant les Cahiers de Paul Valéry* III (Paris:
   Editions Universitaires 1967)

Schmidt-Radefeldt, Jürgen *Paul Valéry linguiste dans les 'Cahiers'* (Paris:
   Klincksieck 1970)

Wills, Ludmilla M. *Le Regard contemplatif chez Valéry et Mallarmé*
   (Amsterdam: Rodopi NV 1974)

Yeschua, Silvio *Valéry, le roman et l'oeuvre à faire* (Paris: Minard 1976)

Articles in Periodicals

Bastet, Ned 'Faust et le cycle' in *Entretiens sur Paul Valéry* (La Haye and Paris:
   Mouton 1968)

 – '"Mon Faust," Textes inédits, Quatrième acte de "Lust"' in *Cahiers Paul
   Valéry II – 'Mes Théâtres'* (Paris: Gallimard 1977)

Brée, Germaine 'The Break-up of Traditional Genres: Bataille, Leiris,
   Michaud,' *Bucknell Review* XXI (Fall-Winter 1973)

Celeyrette-Pietri, Nicole 'Le Jeu du Je' in *Paul Valéry Contemporain* (Paris:
   Klincksieck 1974)

 – '"Au Commencement sera le sommeil": quelques réflections sur un
   poème en prose' in *Cahiers Paul Valéry I – Poétique et poésie* (Paris:
   Gallimard 1975)

Cohn, Robert Greer 'The A B C's of Poetry,' *Comparative Literature* 2 (1962)

Franklin, Ursula 'A Dialectical Triad of Three Early Prose Poems by Paul
   Valéry: "Les Vieilles Ruelles," "Pages Inédites," and "Purs Drames",' to
   appear in *Kentucky Romance Quarterly*

 – 'Mallarméan Affinities in an Early Prose Poem by Paul Valéry,' *The
   French Review* XI 2 (1977)

 – 'The White Night of *Agathe*: A Fragment by Paul Valéry,' *Essays in French
   Literature* 12 (1975)

Levaillant, Jean 'Paul Valéry et la lumière,' *Association Internationale des
   Etudes françaises*, Cahiers 22 (mai 1968)

Nadal, Octave 'Purs Drames,' *Cahiers du Sud* (avril 1957)

Thibaudeau, Jean 'Le Roman comme autobiographie' in *Tel Quel: Théorie
   d'ensemble* (Paris: Editions du Seuil 1968)

Toesca, Maurice 'Paul Valéry: *Agathe' Nouvelle Revue Francaise* (mai 1957)
Yeschua, Silvio 'Substitutions et poétique chez Valéry' in *Cahiers Paul Valéry I – Poétique et poésie* (Paris: Gallimard 1975)

Index

NAMES CITED

Apollinaire, Guillaume 143

Basted, Ned ix, 143, 146
Baudelaire, Charles 4, 6, 13, 43, 55,
  133, 143
Benoist, Jean-Marie 146
Benveniste, Emile 123, 124, 146
Berne-Jeffroy 135
Bernard, Suzanne 3, 133
Brée, Germaine 133

Celeyrette-Pietri, Nicole ix, 137, 144
Cohn, Robert Greer ix, 133, 137
Crow, Christine ix, 136, 142
Culler, Jonathan 146

Dante 28
Derrida, Jacques 140
Diderot, Denis 108, 144

Faivre, J.-L. 42, 138
Flaubert, Gustave 141

Gide, André 5, 10, 11, 17, 18, 47,
  134, 135, 144

Goncourt, Edmond et Jules de 44,
  126

Heredia, J.-M. 46
Huysmans, J.-K. 4, 5, 43, 133, 139

Jakobson, Roman 139, 145
Julien-Cain, Lucienne 136
Jung, C.G. 146

Kristeva, Julia 133

Larbaud, Valery 145
Laurenti, Huguette ix, 138, 139, 144
Laurette, Pierre 145
Lawler, James R. ix, 134, 135, 138
Lebey, Edouard 25, 135
Levaillant, Jean ix, 138
Lussy, Florence de 134

Mallarmé, Stéphane 4, 5, 6, 10, 11,
  12, 14, 16, 17, 18, 19, 41, 43, 44, 46,
  125, 134, 135, 141, 143

Nadal, Octave ix, 10, 133, 134
Neumann, Erich 146

Perse, Saint-Jean 139

Petrarch 28
Plato 11, 13
Poe, Edgar Allan 10, 13, 134

Raymond, Marcel 138, 141
Rimbaud, Arthur 4, 10, 11, 12, 17,
    19, 82, 125, 133, 134, 140, 141
Robinson, Judith ix, 47, 133, 139,
    142, 144
La Rochefoucault, Edméé de 136

Schmidt-Radefeldt, Jürgen 135,
    144

Theocritus 85
Thibaudeau, Jean 122, 145
Toesca, Maurice 81, 144

Vergil 86
Verlaine, Paul 4

Wills, Ludmilla M. 138

Yeschua, Silvio 141, 145

UNIVERSITY OF TORONTO ROMANCE SERIES

1 Guido Cavalcanti's Theory of Love
  J.E. Shaw
2 Aspects of Racinian Tragedy
  John C. Lapp
3 The Idea of Decadence in French Literature, 1830-1900
  A.E. Carter
4 Le Roman de Renart dans la littérature française et dans les
  littératures étrangères au moyen âge
  John Flinn
5 Henry Céard: Idéaliste détrompé
  Ronald Frazee
6 La Chronique de Robert de Clari: Etude de la langue et du style
  P.F. Dembowski
7 Zola before the Rougon-Macquart
  John C. Lapp
8 The Idea of Art as Propaganda in France, 1750-1759:
  A Study in the History of Ideas
  J.A. Leith
9 Marivaux
  E.J.H. Greene
10 Sondages, 1830-1848: Romanciers français secondaires
  John S. Wood
11 The Sixth Sense: Individualism in French Poetry, 1686-1760
  Robert Finch
12 The Long Journey: Literary Themes of French Canada
  Jack Warwick
13 The Narreme in the Medieval Romance Epic:
  An Introduction to Narrative Structures
  Eugene Dorfman
14 Verlaine: A Study in Parallels
  A.E. Carter
15 An Index of Proper Names in
  French Arthurian Verse Romances, 1150-1300
  G.D. West
16 Emery Bigot: Seventeenth-Century French Humanist
  Leonard E. Doucette
17 Diderot the Satirist:
  An Analysis of Le Neveu de Rameau and Related Works
  Donal O'Gorman

18 'Naturalisme pas mort':
Lettres inédites de Paul Alexis à Emile Zola 1871-1900
B.H. Bakker

19 Crispin Ier: La Vie et l'oeuvre de Raymond Poisson,
comédien-poète du xviie siècle
A. Ross Curtis

20 Tuscan and Etruscan:
The Problem of Linguistic Substratum Influence in Central Italy
Herbert J. Izzo

21 Fécondité d'Emile Zola: Roman à thèse, évangile, mythe
David Baguley

22 Charles Baudelaire. Edgar Allan Poe: Sa Vie et ses ouvrages
W.T. Bandy

23 Paul Claudel's Le Soulier de Satin:
A Stylistic, Structuralist, and Psychoanalytic Interpretation
Joan Freilich

24 Balzac's Recurring Characters
Anthony R. Pugh

25 Morality and Social Class in
Eighteenth-Century French Literature and Painting
Warren Roberts

26 The Imagination of Maurice Barrès
Philip Ouston

27 La Cité idéale dans Travail d'Emile Zola
F.I. Case

28 Critical Approaches to Rubén Darío
Keith Ellis

29 Universal Language Schemes in England and France 1600-1800
James Knowlson

30 Science and the Human Comedy:
Natural Philosophy in French Literature from Rabelais to Maupertuis
Harcourt Brown

31 Molière: An Archetypal Approach
Harold C. Knutson

32 Blaise Cendrars: Discovery and Re-creation
Jay Bochner

33 Francesco Guicciardini: The Historian's Craft
Mark Phillips

34 Les Débuts de la lexicographie française:
Estienne, Nicot et le Thresor de la langue françoyse (1606)
T.R. Wooldridge

35 **An Index of Proper Names in French Arthurian Prose Romances**
   G.D. West
36 **The Legendary Sources of Flaubert's** *Saint Julien*
   B.F. Bart and R.F. Cook
37 **The Rule of Metaphor:**
   Multi-disciplinary Studies of the Creation of Meaning in Language
   Paul Ricoeur
38 **The Rhetoric of Valéry's Prose** *Aubades*
   Ursula Franklin

This book
was designed by
ANTJE LINGNER
University of
Toronto
Press